Sharon
Butterfat

PACIFIC POTTERY

JEFFREY B. SNYDER

4880 Lower Valley Road, Atglen, PA 19310 USA

Library of Congress Cataloging-in-Publication Data

Snyder, Jeffrey B.
Pacific pottery / Jeffrey B. Snyder.
p. cm.
1. Pacific Clay Products (Firm)--Catalogs. 2. Ceramic tableware--Collectors and collect-
ing--California--Catalogs. 3. Ceramic tableware--California--History--20th century--
Catalogs. I. Title.
NK4210.P28 A4 2001
738.3'09794'94075--dc21
00-012843

Designed by Bonnie M. Hensley
Cover design by Bruce M. Waters
Type set in Americana XBd BT/Humanist521 BT

ISBN: 0-7643-1276-6
Printed in China
1 2 3 4

Published by Schiffer Publishing Ltd.
4880 Lower Valley Road
Atglen, PA 19310
Phone: (610) 593-1777; Fax: (610) 593-2002
E-mail: Schifferbk@aol.com
Please visit our web site catalog at **www.schifferbooks.com**
We are always looking for people to write books on new and related subjects. If you
have an idea for a book please contact us at the above address.

This book may be purchased from the publisher.
Include $3.95 for shipping.
Please try your bookstore first.
You may write for a free catalog.

In Europe, Schiffer books are distributed by
Bushwood Books
6 Marksbury Ave.
Kew Gardens
Surrey TW9 4JF England
Phone: 44 (0)20-8392-8585
Fax: 44 (0)20-8392-9876
E-mail: Bushwd@aol.com
Free postage in the UK. Europe: air mail at cost

To Naomi Murdach, without whom this book would never have come to be. Thank you Naomi for all your time, hard work, friendly advice, and for your introductions to so many other wonderful people.

ACKNOWLEDGMENTS

I wish to acknowledge everyone who contributed to this book. You were all very generous with your time, your collections, and your information. I could not have done this without you and truly appreciate your efforts, your contributions, and your patience—both during the long hours of the photo shoots and as you awaited the final printing of this book. I am truly grateful!

Special thanks to Naomi and Steven Wybenga of "Naomi's of San Francisco," 1817 Polk Street, San Francisco, California 94109, 417-775-1207.

Special thanks to Peter S. Amantea, Dennis Canavan, Jimm Edgar & Bettie Dakotah, Bill Harmon (Nine Lives Antiques), Rick Hudson ("Hudson's," Berkeley, California), "Jamie" (Star Antiques of San Francisco), Jerry Kunz, Bill Noonan, Robert R. Perry, June Sakata Scoggins, Walter Schirra Ceramics (calpottery@ mindspring.com), Steven H. Schwartz & Casey Hale, Ken Solus & Larry Holben, Bill Stern (wbstern@aol.com), Steve Temme & Dan Craver, Wm. Warmboe Antiques of Burlingame, California, and Mark Wiskow & Susan Strommer (Twentieth Century Styles, 5214 F Diamond Heights #302, San Francisco, California 94131, e-mail tcstyles@aol.com).

I would also like to take a moment and thank Jack Chipman, a pioneering scholar in the field of California pottery. Mr. Chipman has blazed a trail the rest of us follow.

Thanks to the talented staff at Schiffer Publishing as well, who helped pull this book together in its final form and make it beautiful. A very special thank you to Donna Baker, who has willingly edited *yet another* ceramics book!

Finally, I want to thank the readers. Your interest and your input keep these books alive.

CONTENTS

INTRODUCTION

From circa 1916 through 1942, the Pottery Division of the prolific Pacific Clay Products of Los Angeles, California, manufactured a wide range of ceramic wares ranging from early poultry feeders and utilitarian crocks to colorful dinnerwares and stylish artwares. While other divisions produced architectural brick, tile, and sewer pipe for the building trade, this book remains firmly focused on the useful and decorative ceramics made predominantly for the home and garden. Further, the tablewares, kitchenwares, and artwares introduced to the public in 1932 and manufactured for a decade are the "crown jewels" of Pacific's Pottery Division and, as such, will receive the closest attention.

Beautiful examples of Pacific's colorful wares. These items include 9 oz. ball tumbers (catalog #419), 5" h.; a 3 qt. ball jug (catalog #420), 9" h.; and a tray (catalog #452), 16" d. *Courtesy of Robert R. Perry.* Tumblers: $55+ each; jug: $125; tray: $150

When Pacific entered the table and kitchenwares market in earnest in 1932, their wares featured smooth, Art Deco styling adorned with vibrant, solid colored glazes sure to catch the eye. These were durable wares suitable for every day use, yet stylish enough to serve the guests. Furthermore, such wares were craze resistant and oven-proof, and the majority of the kitchenware could be brought from the kitchen directly to the table without embarrassing the host and hostess. These features, and a modest price, were everything a Depression era family could ask for in a quality tableware. The tableware line that made the greatest impact on the public and for which Pacific is most readily recognized today is the Hostess Ware line. As will soon be apparent, Hostess Ware included tablewares, kitchenwares, serving sets, coffee and tea services, punch sets, and martini and canapé sets—a little something for every occasion.

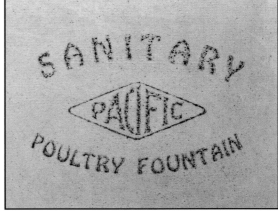

"The Pottery Division of the prolific Pacific Clay Products Company made a wide range of ceramic wares ranging from chicken feeders and utilitarian crocks . . ."
Poultry fountains and feeders, 9", 7", 5.5" h. *Courtesy of June Sakata Scoggins*. These fountain and feeders range in value from $55 to $95.

Among Pacific's early useful wares were this milk pan measuring 13.5" in diameter and these three crocks measuring 8.25", 7", and 7" in diameter. *Courtesy of June Sakata Scoggins*. Milk pan: $125. The crocks range in value from $45 to $85.

" . . . to colorful dinnerwares and stylish artwares."
This "Sunday Supper Set" includes a tray (#452), large bean pot (#232), and individual casseroles or bakers (#205); all are either marked with a circular "Pacific Made In USA" mark or unmarked. Tray, 16" d. *Courtesy of Robert R. Perry.* Tray: $150+; bean pot: $95+; casseroles/bakers: $45 each with lid

Beautiful artware vases, predominantly from the 1930s.
Top: Orange vase with three handles (catalog #800), 6" h.; yellow two handled vase (marked with an incised 21), 4.5" h.; a small blue vase (marked with an incised 34-W), 4.75" h.; a small, early green and black glazed vase (no number), c. 1920s, 3.75" h.
Bottom: large cobalt jardiniere with a circular Pacific mark (most often found in white and pale green), c. 1940s, 5.75" h.; orange vase with molded loop handles and no mark, 5" h.; cobalt vase, c. 1940s, 5.75" h.
Courtesy of Walter Schirra Ceramics (calpottery@mindspring.com). Top, left to right: $150, $250, $250, $150.
Bottom, left to right: $95 each

Two fine examples of later Pacific artware Art Deco style vases with nudes, 15.25" and 14.75" h. *Courtesy of June Sakata Scoggins.* $400+ each

Pacific Clay Products' baseball team, c. 1937. The company's wide range of products are listed on the backs of the players' shirts. Back row, left to right: Quarry Tile, Coralitos Ware, Hostess Ware, Gas Flue, Arcadia Ware, Fire Brick, and Sewer Pipe. Front row, left to right: Power Duct, Flue Lining, Face Brick, Pastel Tile, and Ceramicweld Pipe. *Courtesy of Bill Noonan Collection.*

Artwares, garden pots, and florist wares (in the form of attractive flower pots, frogs, and planters) extended Pacific's range of wares, insinuating themselves throughout the home and out into the yard. When offered in 1932, these too bore bright glazes sure to enliven the home and lift spirits during difficult times. As the decade progressed, women's fashions and tastes turned to pastel colors and Pacific followed suit. The company's wares kept up with the times until America entered the Second World War. In 1942, Pacific Clay Products left behind the production of domestic pottery to support the war effort.

Hostess Ware included tablewares, kitchenwares, serving sets, coffee and tea services, punch sets, and martini and canapé sets—a little something for every occasion. Yellow Hostess Ware place setting: 11", 9.25", 7.5", 6.5" d. plates. *Courtesy of Robert R. Perry.* $10 to $125+ each depending on the piece.

Oval Hostess Ware platters (#444) glazed in orange (beneath the covered oval bowl), cobalt, and yellow, 13 7/8" l.; small oval open vegetable dishes (#494— very scarce), 9.25" l.; divided oval vegetable dish (#640), 12" l.; and an oval bowl in orange, 12" w., with a very rare oval lid (#640-C), 10.5" w. *Courtesy of Mark Wiskow & Susan Strommer.* #444 platters: $125 each; #494 open vegetables: $65 each; #640 divided vegetable: $95+

Left: Hostess Ware after dinner coffee pot (#442) marked "Pacific Made In USA 442," 9.25" h. *Courtesy of Ken Solus & Larry Holben.* $225

Right: Hostess Ware Martini server (#630), with a molded catalog number "630" on the base, 10.25" h. An advertisement in a 1935 *House & Garden* magazine described a set featuring the martini server as including, "A stirring cup to please the most exacting. Full quart in size and complete with a chromium spoon. Individual canapé tray with convenient handle and fitted for cocktail cups. In six Pacific colors." *Courtesy of Robert R. Perry.* $350+

Two example of canapé trays with cocktail cups—only one example featuring the "convenient handle." The tab handled tray measures 7.5" across the tab; the cocktail cup measures 2.25" high. Tray and cup: $135+ per set

While Pacific Clay Products never returned to the production of tablewares, kitchenwares, and artwares, the company did survive the difficult war years. As of this writing, the firm is located in Lake Elsinore, California, and produces architectural wares including custom designed bricks, architectural tiles, and heavy, rolled-rim, terra cotta indoor and outdoor garden pots in "Grand Canyon" and "Tuscany" series, ranging in size from 14.5" to 26.5".

Artwares, garden pots, and florist wares extended Pacific's range of wares, insinuating themselves throughout the home and out into the yard. Three artware vases and a bud vase: white amphora type vase (#812), 11.75" h.; green vase (#873), 10.25" h.; vase (#879), 8" h.; bud vase (#886— a later piece with a circular "Pacific Made in USA" mark), 7.25" h. *Courtesy of Walter Schirra Ceramics (calpottery@mindspring.com).* Left to right: $125, $125, $95, $55

Floor vases, 18" and 16" h. *Courtesy of Robert R. Perry.* $650+ each

Organization

This book begins with a brief overview of the manufacturing processes involved in creating Pacific's pottery. An understanding of these processes both deepens a collector's appreciation for the objects at hand and, more practically, helps to distinguish between marks left on a pot by the manufacturing process and damage subsequently incurred.

Immediately following this overview is an examination of the manufacturer's marks to be found on Pacific pottery and the various marks' approximate periods of use as indicated by the wares they are associated with. With this information, not only will the collector be able to easily identify the company's marked wares, but the astute collector is given a quick way to separate earlier wares from their later brethren, even for pieces that are part of the same line. At times, additional examples of these marks will be shown in association with the wares they are found upon. This way, marks found with a particular line and period will be more firmly associated in the mind.

Next, the book combines the company's history with the wares produced, displaying the wares as they are chronicled in the history of the firm. In this way, the wares are closely identified with their periods of production and the history of the firm is given a more engaging treatment, spread out across the length of the book. The company's early offerings prior to and at the time of the company's entrance into the tableware and artware market in 1932 are dealt with together, as they are more limited in scope. Beginning with the tableware lines and artwares launched after Pacific's 1932 entrance into the domestic market in earnest, the book divides itself between the tablewares and the artwares, presenting the tablewares first as these are the items most readily found by collectors.

A table set with a wide variety of Pacific's Hostess Ware pieces in two complimentary glaze colors. Pacific Clay Products emphasized that their wares were advertised in national magazines and were sold in art and department stores . . . not chains and other discount shops like some of their *East Coast* competitors. Marshall Fields & Company advertisement from *House and Garden* magazine, October 1935. *Courtesy of Bill Harmon, Nine Lives Antiques.*

A Pacific advertisement dating from around 1937. It reads: "In Colors from an Artist's Palette. Pacific Hostess Ware, Coralitos Dinnerware, Pacific Artware. Pacific pottery offers you a choice of sixteen beautiful colors from which to select your table and artwares. Illustrated on the right are some of the outstanding pieces of Pacific Hostess Ware, one of the first of today's brilliant potteries to interpret the mood of colorful California. Ask to be shown the many attractive and unusual pieces not pictured." *Courtesy of Bill Harmon, Nine Lives Antiques.*

Pricing

The prices found in the captions are in United States dollars. Prices vary immensely based on the location of the market, the venue of the sale, the rarity of the items and/or their glaze treatments, and the enthusiasms of the collecting community. Items in rare glaze colors may far exceed the prices for identical wares in more common colors. With this in mind, many prices are followed by a "+" sign, reminding the reader that such rarities may exceed the values given. Prices in the Midwest differ from those in the West or East, and those at specialty shows or auctions will differ from those in dealer's shops or through dealer's web pages.

All of these factors make it impossible to create absolutely accurate price listings, but a guide to realistic pricing may be offered. **Please note:** these values are not provided to set prices in the antiques marketplace, but rather to give the reader a reasonable idea of what one might expect to pay for mint condition Pacific wares.

MANUFACTURING PACIFIC POTTERY & MANUFACTURER'S MARKS

Manufacturing Processes

This "Pacific Pottery from California" advertisement describes the character and colors of Hostess Ware. It reads, "Gray Winter Days Ahead. Enliven your home with Color. With winter just around the corner, all outdoors dons its soberest dress. Color and warmth move inside; the home becomes once more the center of conviviality. Emphasize this gayer feeling in your home with Pacific Pottery. All the lush tones of the mountains, the desert, and the sea, are caught on its smooth glazes, and our designers have tried to anticipate your every serving need. There are many clever new pieces for informal buffet suppers, complete services for colorful breakfasts, lunches, dinners. While our baking dishes, with their new, detachable wooden handles, have become so very beautiful, they refuse to stay in the kitchen. Now they join the others at the table. All of these fascinating pieces come in the six Pacific colors, Lemon Yellow, Apache Red, Pacific Blue, Sierra White, Jade Green, and Delphinium Blue. . . . Three pieces from our new baking contingent. Open baker, pie plate, and covered casserole large enough for turkey. The detachable wooden handles are exclusive with Pacific. Pacific Pottery From California. Division of Pacific Clay Products, Los Angeles Calif." *Courtesy of Bill Harmon, Nine Lives Antiques.*

GRAY WINTER DAYS AHEAD *Enliven your home with Color*

With winter just around the corner, all outdoors dons its soberest dress. Color and warmth move inside; the home becomes once more the center of conviviality. Emphasize this gayer feeling in your home with Pacific Pottery. All the lush tones of the mountains, the desert and the sea, are caught in its smooth glazes, and our designers have tried to anticipate your every serving need. There are many clever new pieces for informal buffet suppers,

complete services for colorful breakfasts, lunches, dinners. While our baking dishes, with their new, detachable wooden handles, have become so very beautiful, they refuse to stay in the kitchen. Now they join the others at the table. All of these fascinating pieces come in the six Pacific colors, Lemon Yellow, Apache Red, Pacific Blue, Sierra White, Jade Green, and Delphinium Blue. *Sold at leading stores. Descriptive folder available upon request.*

Three pieces from our new baking contingent. Open baker, pie plate, and covered casserole large enough for turkey. The detachable, wooden handles are exclusive with Pacific.

Pacific POTTERY
FROM CALIFORNIA
Division of PACIFIC CLAY PRODUCTS, Los Angeles, Calif.

Terminology

Before moving on to Pacific's manufacturing techniques, it will be useful to discuss a few general terms. In 1935, Pacific's dinnerware, kitchenware, and artware products were described in the *Ceramic Industry* trade journal as being made with a strong stoneware body prepared from a carefully controlled mixture of five different clays mined from five different regions within California. Stoneware is a rugged, hard, high-fired ceramic body that is both opaque and non-porous. The kiln heat is high enough to vitrify the body material, giving it a glass-like quality that renders it impenetrable by liquids. Unglazed stoneware bodies are usually gray, buff, or brown in color. A wide variety of glaze colors were employed over time to give these stonewares a more appealing look.

Some of Pacific Clay Products' early 1920s utilitarian wares have been described as yellow wares. Yellow wares are porous earthenwares with yellow-gold or buff-yellow bodies. Yellow wares require a glaze coating to become impermeable to liquids. Yellow wares were primarily produced as kitchenwares and chamber pots in America between roughly 1830 and 1930.

Glaze is actually a clear glass-like coating to which various metallic oxides are added to impart different colors to the glazes. When applied to non-porous stonewares, glazes are used to give them a bright, smooth surface. However, in the case of lower fired, and porous earthenware ceramic bodies (such as yellow wares), glazes are used to seal the earthenware against liquids, which would otherwise be absorbed into the ceramic as well.

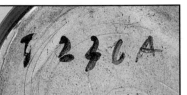

This vase is decorated in a rare purple test glaze. A hand painted test glaze number designation, "T236A," is marked on the base. 11.25" h. *Courtesy of June Sakata Scoggins.* $650

Early yellow ware mixing bowls ranging in size from 16" to 6" in diameter and stamped in black ink with diamond shaped "Pacific" marks. Nine bowls are shown in this photograph. *Courtesy of June Sakata Scoggins.* These mixing bowls range in value by size from $75 to $235.

Pottery Manufacturing

Prior to the production of a new Pacific line, members of both the design and sales staffs were likely to have put their heads together with management to generate ideas for future Pacific lines. Once a list of ideas was in hand, it would be up to the design department to determine both which designs *should* be developed and which designs *could* be successfully developed and manufactured within the plant. This initial determination might narrow a list of twenty-five potential designs to twelve feasible designs. The most popular of the feasible designs would then be selected by the designers.

Once a design was selected, it was first modeled in plaster. The plaster model produced was some fifteen percent larger than the eventual product, to account for the inevitable shrinkage that would occur between the molding of the object and its final run through the fires of the kiln. If the plaster model was to feature additional ornamentation, such adornments were rendered in a non-drying oil modeling clay and added to the model. These additional decorative features were also produced over-sized, of course.

When the model met the designer's specifications and was accepted, a mold was made from the model. At this point, the model was destroyed and the mold was then used to create a "reverse mold" (an object cast from that first mold that acts as a model) from which additional molds would be cast. Depending on the anticipated popularity of the object, anywhere from 100 to 1000 molds might be produced.

As the molds were being developed, five clays from different regions of California were being processed and impurities in the clays eliminated; the five were then mixed to create the clay base necessary to successfully produce the new Pacific product. To ensure that shrinkage was limited (beyond a certain point shrinkage creates cracks in a clay body that destroy the piece), some previously fired clay (bisque) was ground into a fine powder and added to the mix. The addition of the fired clay both reduced the total shrink rate and improved the overall quality of the clay body.

Once the clay was prepared and the molds were ready, flat wares (plates, platters, and such) were jiggered, cups were jollyed, and many hollow forms (pitchers, vases, and various artwares) were slip cast. (However, please note that Pacific's early artware vases (c. 1920s-early 1930s) were hand thrown rather than slip cast.) Jiggering used a soft, pliable clay cut into flat disks, jollying involved the use of soft clay balls, and slip casting used liquid clay.

To manufacture a plate, the jigger man would place a clay disk over a mold on the rotating jigger wheel. The mold formed the interior surface of the plate (upon which food would eventually rest) while a tool was used to sculpt the plate's underside.

Once the clay was prepared and the molds were ready, flat wares were jiggered, cups were jollyed, and many hollow forms were slip cast. Three quart pitcher (#508) with lid, 8.25" h.; six footed goblets (#433) in orange, cobalt, yellow, white, green, 5.5" h. and Delphinium blue; and a two ring cake plate in white, 13" d. *Courtesy of Mark Wiskow & Susan Strommer.* Pitcher: $225; goblets: $125+ each; cake plate: $195

However, Pacific's early artware vases (c. 1920s-early 1930s) were hand thrown rather than slip cast. Vase (#19), marked with an incised "19," 5.75" h. *Courtesy of June Sakata Scoggins.* $275+

Prototype vase with experimental green glaze, incised ring decoration, marked "T-82," 4.75" h. *Courtesy of Jimm Edgar & Bettie Dakotah.* $300+

Vase, incised "C," 5.25" h. *Courtesy of June Sakata Scoggins.* $250+

Vase, incised "19," 5.75" h. *Courtesy of June Sakata Scoggins.* $175+

To produce a cup, the jiggerman pushed an appropriately shaped profile tool down into a clay ball packed into a rotating mold affixed to the turning jiggering wheel. The mold shaped the cup's exterior as the tool formed the cup's interior. With the jigger wheel rotating 200 times a minute, a cup or plate was formed in a matter of seconds.

From the jiggering wheel, jiggered and jollyed pieces were taken, still in the mold, to a drying room. A combination of heat from the room and the absorbent nature of the plaster mold dried each piece in about two hours.

To slip cast hollow wares, liquid clay (or slip) was poured into the open top of a mold. Depending on the thickness required for the finished piece, the slip was allowed to stand in the mold anywhere from thirty minutes to two hours. The longer the slip sat, the more slip would adhere to the mold walls, increasing the thickness of the piece. When the time was right and the piece was deemed thick enough, the remaining liquid slip was poured out of the mold. Once the liquid slip was gone, the plaster mold would draw moisture out of the remaining clay until the molded piece separated itself from the mold walls. Once the molded clay was free of the mold walls, the piece was removed.

Handles, spouts, and finials were cast in separate molds. These were then applied to the pieces needing them. They were attached to the molded clay bodies with slip. When later fired, the separate pieces became integral parts of the pottery, as firmly attached as if they had been molded as parts of the piece itself.

Handles, spouts, and finials were cast in separate molds and attached to the bodies with clay slip. Six cup Hostess Ware teapot (#447), sugar bowl (#463), and creamer (#464). *Courtesy of June Sakata Scoggins.* Teapot: $195; sugar and creamer: $75 set

At this point, women carefully inspected the "green" (unfired) pottery. They trimmed away excess clay and rubbed the areas smooth with damp sponges. Once the pottery had passed inspection and sat for about 24 hours, gaining a leathery texture, it was sent on to the glazing department. For Pacific, as for many major California potteries of the 1930s, glazes were applied prior to the firing of the clay bodies. Using a single fire process (instead of firing the clay into a bisque state, adding glaze to the bisque, and firing again) fused the glaze to the clay, greatly reducing the chance for crazing. Crazing occurred when the clay body shrank over time after firing. Glaze being a hard, glassy coating, it could not shrink along with the body beneath it. As a result, the glaze would crack, creating fine, spidery lines across the surface of the piece.

As described in *California—Magazine of Pacific Business*, glaze itself is a highly refined liquid clay mixed with finely ground metal oxides. Different metal oxides gave the glaze different colors. (1937, p. 41) Both copper oxides and cobalt created blues; chromium oxides made greens; manganese oxides produced browns, tans, and greens; uranium yielded orange, yellows, and Chinese red; and tin provided whites. At Pacific, during the 1930s, the company's chemist John Lathrop devised the firm's colorful glazes under the watchful eye of the plant superintendent, C. Friederichsen. (Kaeppel 1938, p. 62)

At Pacific, during the 1930s, John Lathrop devised the company's colorful glazes. Hostess Ware salt (#620) and pepper (#621) shakers in a low artware bowl (#854). The bowl measures 12" d. x 2" h. *Courtesy of June Sakata Scoggins.* Shakers: $25+ each; artware bowl: $55

Items that would drain evenly, such as tumblers, were simply dipped into glazes. Objects that would not drain well, such as chop plates, were sprayed. Whether sprayed or dipped, the glaze coating had to be consistent, as glaze colors varied with the thickness of the coating.

Once the glaze coat was successfully applied to the body of any vessel, some method was needed to keep the glaze from hardening to the sagger (a protective clay box into which pottery was placed) during kiln firing. Two common ways to keep the glaze out of contact with the sagger involve using either a dry foot or a stilt. A "foot" is a base upon which a ceramic object rests. Using the dry foot method, workers carefully removed any traces of glaze from the foot prior to firing, ensuring that the foot would be "dry" when fired, thus preventing glaze from adhering to the sagger.

The feet on this syrup pitcher (#435) illustrate the dry foot technique. *Courtesy of Robert R. Perry.*

If the bottom of a piece was to be glazed, then the glazed base could be kept out of contact with the sagger by using stilts. A stilt is a small, Y shaped bisque support, a type of "kiln furniture," with projections reaching up above and down below the Y. A pot may be placed on the stilt's projecting ends, keeping the glazed base raised up off the sagger. During firing, as the glaze hardens, it adheres to both the pot and the stilt tips at those three small points. Once the firing is complete, and the object cooled, it is a simple matter to give the pot a quick twist to snap it free from the bisque stilt. Remnants of the stilt tips adhering to the pot were then ground down, leaving behind three glaze-free dots marking the spots where the stilt supported the piece. These are called "stilt marks" and should not be mistaken for damage. Very large pieces may have more than three stilt marks. In the 1930s, metal stilts were developed that eliminated the need for grinding stilt fragments from vessel bases but did not eliminate the stilt marks.

More than three glazeless spots may appear on larger pieces requiring greater support, such as this circular tab handled tray. *Courtesy of Walter Schirra Ceramics (calpottery@mindspring.com).*

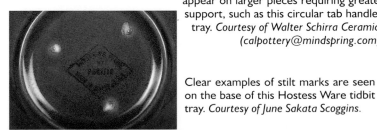

Clear examples of stilt marks are seen on the base of this Hostess Ware tidbit tray. *Courtesy of June Sakata Scoggins.*

23

Molded, glazed, and placed within saggers, pottery was now ready to pass through the kiln (furnace), fusing the glaze to the body and hardening both into their final forms. When Pacific began making dinnerware and artware in their Lincoln Heights plant (one of several owned by the company), the company equipped the former Los Angeles Stoneware Company site with a modern gas fired tunnel kiln. That kiln was not only capable of firing all the artware and dinnerware desired, but could also handle architectural terra cotta, electrical porcelain, glazed brick, and any other building product the company chose to produce.

The tunnel kiln had distinct advantages over the older "beehive" kilns. Beehive kilns took anywhere from days to weeks to be loaded, fired, cooled, and emptied of a load of pottery. Tunnel kilns finished the job in as little as 18 hours. Tunnel kilns also rolled the pottery through its depths on a continuous conveyor and cooled the pottery before its left the kiln's 150 foot length. Pottery moved through the kiln constantly, providing a much greater output than its beehive shaped predecessors.

During the firing, it was essential that the tunnel kiln temperature remained constant. A combination of electronic devices and clay cones were used to keep an eye on the temperature. While the electronics checked the heat every twenty seconds and increased or decreased the gas flames as needed, refined clay cones provided the operator with a visual check of his own. These cones were placed along the conveyor line on the saggers at regular intervals. Different cones had different melting points. If certain cones melted, the kiln was too hot, while if others did *not* melt, the kiln was too cool.

The reason for the constant vigilance in regards to the heat of the kiln had to do with glaze colors. If the kiln was too hot, glaze colors changed. Orange glazes turned black around the edges, for example, and turquoise turned blue if the kiln was ten to fifteen degrees too hot. A ruby red glaze was affected by as little as a two degree variance!

The far end of the tunnel kiln was designed to cool the pottery. Once the pottery had passed through the kiln, it was ready to be unloaded, inspected, and shipped. Around 1938, Pacific added an electric decorating kiln they designed themselves to the plant.

Tell-Tale Marks and Mistakes of Pottery Production

Now that we have reviewed the pottery manufacturing process, it is worth taking a moment to explore some of the more common factory flaws found on ceramics. While these factory flaws tend to lower the value of the pottery upon which they are found, they should not be mistakenly identified as damage inflicted upon the pot at some later date. Pacific Clay Products advertised that they disposed of factory seconds; however, they did sell seconds in a shop on the factory grounds, so examples of these factory mishaps, while limited, should exist.

Common factory flaws include unusual glaze color variations, visible mold seam lines, uneven bases, lids that do not fit properly, and handles that do not match. At times, pottery chipped in the bisque stage was still glazed and fired. On close inspection, you will note in such cases that the glaze completely covers the chip. Finally, "kiln kisses" occur when a pot touches either the sagger wall or another pot as it is being loaded for firing, leaving dents or unglazed areas on the pot.

Note the very clear mold seam line bisecting the middle drink container, a common flaw in molded wares when no one takes the time to smooth the seam lines prior to the ware's firing. Three small early drink containers (orange or lemon) in granite ware and yellow ware bodies, 3.5" to 3.25" h. *Courtesy of June Sakata Scoggins.* $95+ each

Manufacturer's Marks

Manufacturer's marks are generally found on the undersides or backs of ceramics, where they are unobtrusive. These marks may be molded, impressed, incised, or stamped in place. Marks identify pottery as the work of a particular firm. Not every piece produced by a company would be marked. There was little need to mark every piece of a set that was to be sold together. Small pieces were frequently difficult to mark. Items that were produced to be given away as premiums or fair prizes were not necessarily items a company cared to be associated with and were therefore also often left unmarked. Special order items made for a particular client might be left unmarked at the client's request. Pacific also produced a paper label they could use from the 1930s onward in lieu of a manufacturer's mark.

Pacific produced a paper label they could use in lieu of a manufacturer's mark. Pacific Pottery paper label. *Courtesy of Walter Schirra Ceramics (calpottery@mindspring.com).*

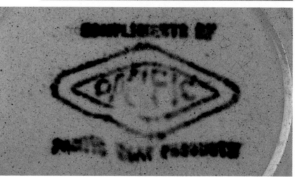

Early rounded diamond shaped Pacific ink stamp marks with a double border were used by the Pacific Clay Products Company/Pacific Clay Products during the 1920s. The mark on the exterior of a stoneware crock reads between the borders "The Pacific Clay Products Inc. Los Angeles." The second mark has printed above and below the mark "Compliments of Pacific Clay Products." This mark was found on an early vase. Two ink stamped marks are also shown on blue banded and blended glaze mixing bowls. A single bordered ink stamped "Pacific" mark was also used during the early years of production (largely prior to the company's entering the tableware/artware market in earnest in 1932). *Courtesy of June Sakata Scoggins; courtesy of Mark Wiskow & Susan Strommer.*

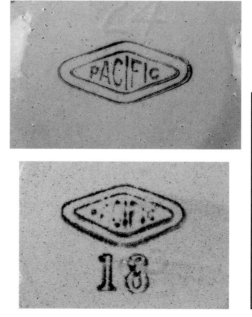

Items that were produced to be given away were not necessarily items a company cared to be associated with. Souvenir wares were likely to be left without manufacturer's marks to identify them. Pacific souvenir hats produced for the "America's Exposition San Diego 1935," otherwise unmarked, 4.25" d. x 2.25" h. *Courtesy of Naomi's of San Francisco.* $165 each

Both impressed and ink stamped diamond shaped Pacific marks with pointed tips were also employed. The impressed diamond shaped, single bordered mark with the #12 catalog number was found on an early dog dish. A diamond shaped ink stamp with sharper edges was stamped on a Saturn bowl (catalog #701), postdating the company's 1932 transition to the tableware/artware market. An impressed diamond shaped mark was also found on an early "plain ware" stein from c. 1932 or beyond. *Courtesy of June Sakata Scoggins; courtesy of Walter Schirra Ceramics (calpottery@mindspring.com).*

The distinctive "PACIFIC" mark featuring a sun over the ocean motif dates from 1932. It marked a medallion reading "X Olympiad 1932-Los Angeles California." The impressed mark, without the rising sun motif, marked a distinctive, round Pacific ashtray featured in an *Arts & Decorations* magazine advertisement dating from April 1935. This impressed PACIFIC mark also appeared on a Hostess Ware oval tray (catalog #444) of roughly the same period. Expect to find a variety of marks on Hostess Ware as this line was a mainstay of the company throughout much, if not all, of this pottery producing decade (1932-1942). *Courtesy of the collection of Steve Temme & Dan Craver; courtesy of Mark Wiskow & Susan Strommer; courtesy of Naomi's of San Francisco.*

As the 1930s progressed, Pacific developed a variety of circular marks, both molded and stamped. The first molded mark reads "PACIFIC MADE IN USA" with the catalog number for the #601 Hostess Ware sauce dish. This mark identified one of the company's decorated wares adorned with the Poppy motif. (This author has seen "Plaid" (BG) decorated wares in a 1935 advertisement and additional decorated wares advertised in 1937. Please note that, throughout the captions, when a name is in quotes, it is the common name given to the piece by present-day collectors. In this case, collectors commonly refer to Pacific's BG pattern as "Plaid.") *Courtesy of Mark Wiskow & Susan Strommer.*

The Coralitos line was new in 1937 and was identified with this circular Pacific mark and the X39 catalog number for the after dinner coffee pot. The Arcadia line was released at roughly the same time as Coralitos. It is interesting to note that this mark replaces the Pacific company name with the Arcadia line name. A shortened version of the circular Pacific mark identifies a late 1930s tab handled vase. *Courtesy of Walter Schirra Ceramics (calpottery@mindspring.com); courtesy of June Sakata Scoggins; courtesy of Robert R. Perry.*

An abbreviated molded "PACIFIC USA" mark identifies this half round planter (catalog #719). As with the circular, molded Pacific marks, this is most likely a mark dating from the latter half of the 1930s. *Courtesy of Robert R. Perry.*

With only the catalog number 3349 and "Made In USA" on this vase, dating from c. 1941-1942, one suspects this mark may have been used for either promotional items or wares made by request for clients who chose not to have the wares associated with the pottery firm. *Courtesy of June Sakata Scoggins.*

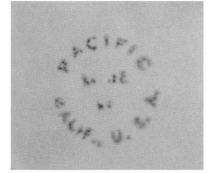

This circular ink stamp mark, reading "Pacific Made In Calif. USA," identified both a ballerina figurine and a bird vase dating from c. 1941-1942. *Courtesy of Walter Schirra Ceramics (calpottery@mindspring.com); courtesy of Jerry Kunz.*

The Dura-Rim line was introduced c. 1940. This blue ink stamped diamond shaped mark reads "Dura-Rim by Pacific Made in Calif. USA." Similar marks replacing the Dura-Rim name with Hostess Ware and Art Ware date from the same period. *Courtesy of Walter Schirra Ceramics (calpottery@mindspring.com); courtesy of June Sakata Scoggins.*

The scenic ink stamped rectangular mark features a central scene of the California coast. Above the rectangle, the mark reads "Pacific." Below the rectangle, the mark reads "Hand Painted/Made in California/Pat. Pend. USA." The first mark is also identified as a "Sample" designation in red on one side, indicating that this is a sample vase the company made to show to potential buyers and/or to pass through management's ranks for approval prior to mass production. This mark is also conveniently dated September 17, 1941. The second, clearer version of this rectangular mark appears on a California Grape pattern hand painted plate. The California Grape pattern was introduced c. 1941 as well. Hand painted, embossed patterns came into vogue around 1940. (The Franciscan Apple pattern, produced by Pacific's competitor Gladding, McBean & Company, was also introduced in that year.) The last two ink stamped marks were also found on California Grape pattern pieces, placing them in the c. 1941 time frame as well. *Courtesy of Bill Stern (wbstern@aol.com); courtesy of June Sakata Scoggins.*

PACIFIC CLAY PRODUCTS
HISTORY AND WARES

Early Wares: c. 1916 - 1932

Pacific Clay Products as a company was created in the merger of several pioneering Southern California pottery enterprises. Near Lake Elsinore, California, the Southern California Coal and Clay Company began manufacturing clay sewer pipe in 1886. In 1887, the firm expanded, building two more plants. Together, these manufactories became the Pacific Clay Manufacturing Company and the California Clay Manufacturing Company. In 1900, the Los Angeles Stoneware Company first organized and opened a pottery along the river in Los Angeles' Lincoln Heights district at West Avenue 26. In 1903, Los Angeles Stoneware's Lincoln Heights plant was purchased by the Douglass Clay Products Company. These disparate enterprises, with factories in Los Angeles, Corona, and Lake Elsinore, merged in 1910, forming the Pacific Sewer Pipe Company. In 1911, Pacific added a plant in Los Nietos, fifteen miles from Los Angeles, while closing the Corona and Elsinore factories. In 1916, the company name was changed to Pacific Clay Products Company. In 1923, the firm was acquired by a new corporation, The Pacific Clay Products, Inc. Under the direction of William Lacy, the firm sought to capitalize on the California building boom of the 1920s, producing a variety of architectural products. In 1925, the company name was shortened to Pacific Clay Products. The center of operations, and the primary site for the creation of dinner, kitchen, and artwares in the 1930s and early 1940s, was based in the pottery factory located in Los Angeles' Lincoln Heights district at 306 West Avenue 26.

The Pacific name originated in 1887 with the Pacific Clay Manufacturing Company. Redware storage jars, 14.25" and 13.75" h. Left marked (incomplete) "PACIFIC MAN'F'G CO. South Riverside CAL." *Courtesy of June Sakata Scoggins.* $145; $125

The fledgling company's early wares included both the aforementioned architectural materials and utilitarian wares useful around the home . . . and in the barn yard. Pacific utilitarian wares were manufactured in terra cotta, yellow ware, and white stonewares described as "sanitary wares." Gleaming white wares had been perceived, since the 1870s among potteries back East, as conveying a greater sense of cleanliness than yellow wares and were also seen as a better canvas upon which to apply a variety of bright glaze colors.

Gleaming white sanitary wares were perceived as conveying a greater sense of cleanliness than yellow wares. White sanitary ware mixing bowls with 3 blue stripes: mixing bowl (#12), 9.25" d.; mixing bowl (#24), 7" d. *Courtesy of Mark Wiskow & Susan Strommer.* #12: $75; #24: $65

Among the early wares were batter and mixing bowls, bean pots, custard cups, dog dishes, tankards and steins (a.k.a. beer mugs), and poultry fountains and feeders. An April 1924 catalog, displaying the "Pacific Clay Products Inc. Stoneware Factory" (306 West Avenue, Los Angeles) site on the cover, listed a stoneware cereal set, patty dishes, beer mugs, and miscellaneous specialties among their wares. The stoneware cereal set included one pitcher, a sugar bowl, and three cereal bowls. In 1924, one hundred of those stoneware beer mugs could be purchased for twenty-five dollars.

With contributions from potter Harold Johnson (with the company until 1928, prior to his move to the Catalina Clay Products pottery company), the firm also produced a number of garden pots and vases to add depth to the pottery line. The company quickly developed a reputation for quality wares that would serve them well in years to come.

Harold Johnson made this vase. It is adorned with an extremely unusual blended lavender and cobalt glaze. *Courtesy of Mark Wiskow & Susan Strommer.* $225+

Glazes utilized by Pacific during the 1920s included orange, green, cobalt, and black. Orange glazed wares were produced in great abundance. Harold Johnson has been credited with the development of Pacific's blended glazes, introduced to the general public around the mid-1920s. Blending the basic glaze colors in a soft, intermingled wash of colors provided a distinctive look sure to attract attention.

Blended glazes were used to finish this mixing bowl and these vases. Mixing bowl (#12), 9.5" d.; narrow necked vase, 8.25" h.; vase, 4.25" h. These pieces are identified with the diamond shaped "Pacific" manufacturer's mark. *Courtesy of June Sakata Scoggins.* Mixing bowl: $195; 8.25" h. vase: $225; 4.25" h. vase: $175

Pacific's 1920s hand thrown artwares (vases and pots) were glazed in orange, cobalt, black, a deep matte green, yellow, and a matte burgundy. Today, collectors will pay more for 1920s artwares or utilitarian wares glazed in any other color than orange. Both cobalt and black are very popular colors among collectors of the early Pacific wares. While artwares tend to bring higher values than the utilitarian wares, very large kitchenware objects will bring the highest prices in most cases. (Wiskow 1999)

From July 27 to September 3, 1928, Pacific Clay Products displayed their wares at the Pacific Southwest Exposition in Long Beach, California. At that exposition, between 30,000 and 80,000 people were exposed to Pacific's pottery (from the 1850s onward, exhibitions, expositions, and world's fairs were wonderful places for manufacturers to familiarize the public with their wares and for observant manufacturers to pick up on new trends in the marketplace). Pacific Clay Products' wares of 1928 were described broadly as including, "various prod-

ucts . . . ranging from utilitarian water coolers to fancy ware." (*Ceramic Industry* 1928)

In April of 1929, company president William Lacy was happy to report that Pacific Clay Products had increased its earnings over the previous year. Looking ahead, however, Mr. Lacy voiced a concern: "In looking forward to 1929, it appears that the total volume of construction work calling for our company's products is likely to be less than in 1928." (*Ceramic Industry* 1929)

William Lacy was correct, more so than he was likely to have realized. When economic depression swept across the nation in 1929, the California building boom ground to a halt. For an American pottery company to survive the Depression years, new product lines would be required.

As an interesting side note, in April of 1929 Pacific's management was also keenly interested in evidence that suggested oil might be found under their Los Nietos, Santa Fe Springs, pottery plant.

Bean Pots, Crocks, Chicken Feeders, Containers, & Dog Bowls

Bean pots, 7.5", 3.75, and 3.5" h.
Courtesy of June Sakata Scoggins.
These bean pots range in value
from $35 to $65.

31

Pacific crocks in sanitary stoneware and yellow ware, 13" h. and 8" h. *Courtesy of June Sakata Scoggins.* $165, $85

Early yellow ware crock with a diamond shaped ink stamped front "Pacific" mark and an impressed "3#" on the base, 6.75" d. *Courtesy of Robert R. Perry.* $45

Pacific crocks, 13.5" to 5" d. The small examples were butter crocks. *Courtesy of June Sakata Scoggins.* These crocks range in value from $45 to $165.

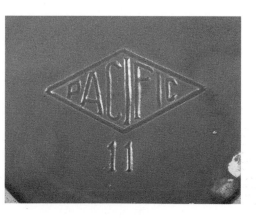

Early Pacific poultry feeder (the base plate is missing), 5.75" h. *Courtesy of Naomi's of San Francisco*. $45 complete

Top right: Two shoulder jugs. The large jug measures 13" high. The 13" h. jug is marked "5" (for 5 gallons). *Courtesy of June Sakata Scoggins.* $125; $55

Bottom center & right: Covered container (#11) molded with a basketweave decoration and a flower finial, impressed with a diamond shaped "Pacific" mark and number, 8.5" h. *Courtesy of June Sakata Scoggins.* $95

Another example of a blended glaze large covered storage container. 10.5" h. x 12.75" d. *Courtesy of Naomi's of San Francisco.* $1150+

Large covered storage container in blended glazes, 10.5" h. x 12.75" d. *Courtesy of June Sakata Scoggins.* $1150+

Unusual blended glazes on a mixing bowl (#12), 9.5" d., and lidded containers (for cigarettes, marmalade?), 3.5" and 2.5" h. These wares were marked with the ink stamped diamond shaped "Pacific" manufacturer's mark. *Courtesy of June Sakata Scoggins.* Mixing bowl: $195; 3.5" h. container: $450+; 2.5" h. container: $350+. The container without the lid is valued at $195.

Blended glaze vase and two covered containers. All are marked with the ink stamped diamond shaped "Pacific" mark. *Courtesy of Naomi's of San Francisco.* Vase: $450+; containers: $350+ each

Blended glaze containers identified with ink stamped Pacific diamond with double line marks, 12.75" and 10" h. *Courtesy of June Sakata Scoggins.* Left to right: $295, $275

Early dog and puppy bowls, relief molded in yellow ware: #12 (tapered), #14 (the largest), and #15 (marked "Puppy" and very rare). #14: 8" x 4.5"; Puppy #15: 6" x 3" h. *Courtesy of June Sakata Scoggins.* Top: #14: $125; #15 "Puppy:" $195+. Bottom: #12: $125 each

The straight sided #14 dog bowl is referred to as the "dog show bowl" by collectors, so called because of the plaques depicted behind the relief molded dogs, 4.5" h. x 8" d.; #12 tapered dog bowl, 3.75" h. x 4.25" d. at opening. *Courtesy of Mark Wiskow & Susan Strommer.* $125 each

Artwares

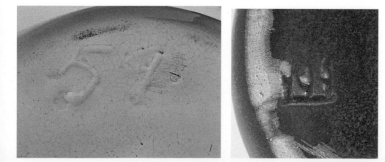

Early hand thrown artware: orange vase featuring rings with burn in the glaze, 11" h.; yellow vase (#59) featuring two ring bands, a spherical form, and a collar, 7.75" h.; spherical vase in cobalt, 5 1/8" h.; spherical vase with collar and rings, incised 18 mark, 5.25" h.; and a small handled vase with an indistinct, incised mark (possibly a # 27), 4.5" h. *Courtesy of Mark Wiskow & Susan Strommer.* Orange vase: $450; # 59 yellow vase: $350+; spherical vase: $250; small handled vase: $250

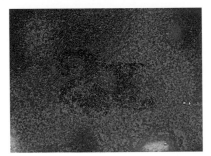

Vase, ink stamp marked "2X," 11.5" h.
Courtesy of June Sakata Scoggins. $350+

Early Pacific vase marked with an "R" by hand on the base. 5" h. *Courtesy of Bill Stern (wbstern@aol.com).* $125

Three early vases by Pacific: left vase, marked in black "#175," with an incised "E;" center and right vases, unmarked. 11", 8.5" & 7" high respectively. *Courtesy of Wm. Warmboe Antiques of Burlingame, California.* Left to right: $650+ (rare purple glaze color), $350+, $365

Vase, incised on the base with a "D." 8" h. *Courtesy of June Sakata Scoggins.* $350+

Two styles of small, early Pacific vases. The first two on the left are in bisque coated in a matte finish without a glossy glaze while the remainder are glazed. All of these vases are unmarked, ranging in size from 4.25" to 4" h. The interiors of the vases reveal different body types, either yellow ware or granite ware (sanitary ware). *Courtesy of June Sakata Scoggins.* $85 each

Three early vases: the black example has an interior rim for a lid. The other two vases have blended glazes. All are unmarked and measure 3.75" high. *Courtesy of June Sakata Scoggins.* $150+ each

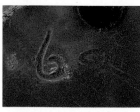

Three vases, early prototypes with hand written notations on the bases and an incised number "64." 14.75" h. *Courtesy of Wm. Warmboe Antiques of Burlingame, California.* Blended glazes: $450+ each; orange glaze: $350+

Identical vases featuring different glaze treatments: blended glaze and green glaze, 8" h. and 8.25" h. *Courtesy of Walter Schirra Ceramics (calpottery@mindspring.com).* Left to right: $225, $195

Vases with blended glazes, 8" and 4.25" h. *Courtesy of June Sakata Scoggins.* Left to right: $225+, $175

Blended glaze decorated vase marked with a stamped diamond shaped "Pacific" mark and "Compliments of Pacific Clay Products," 8" h. *Courtesy of June Sakata Scoggins.* $225

Top left: Two blended glaze vases, marked with a diamond shaped "Pacific" stamp in black, 4" h. *Courtesy of Wm. Warmboe Antiques of Burlingame, California.* $350+ pair

Top right: Blended glaze vase, the yellow ware body under the glaze showing through, 10" h. *Courtesy of June Sakata Scoggins.* $275

Bottom right and center: Low artware bowl marked with an incised "K," 9" d. *Courtesy of June Sakata Scoggins.* $65+

Kitchen & Serving Wares

These items range from custard cups and mixing bowls to steins and tankards.

Blended glazes on two bowls and a flower frog. The Pacific mark inside the bowl may have been used by a salesman in a show. Bowls, 6.75" and 5.25" d. Flower frog, 3.75" d. Only the frog is not marked with the diamond shaped "Pacific" stamped mark. *Courtesy of June Sakata Scoggins.* Bowls: $225+ each; flower frog: $95

A sanitary ware bowl finished with blue and red blended glazes. To find this glaze treatment on sanitary ware, rather than on yellow ware, is very unusual. 5.5" d. x 3" h. *Courtesy of Mark Wiskow & Susan Strommer.* $125+

Early custard cups. The top cup is ink stamp marked on the front "Pacific Sewer Pipe Co. Los Angeles" (c. 1910-1915) under the glaze. One cup is also ink stamp marked with the diamond shaped "Pacific" manufacturer's mark. 4" d. x 2.5" h. each. *Courtesy of June Sakata Scoggins.* Top: $50; bottom: $20+

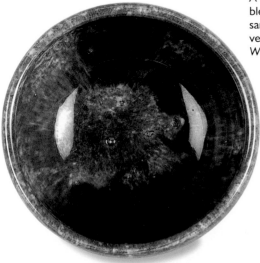

45

Two early yellow ware custard cups with stamped "Pacific" diamond shaped marks. The right hand example has a doubled bordered mark. 4" and 3.75" d. *Courtesy of June Sakata Scoggins.* $30 each

Early custard cups produced in yellow ware, black glazing, yellow ware with overglaze decorations added after the piece left the factory, and a blended orange and red glaze. *Courtesy of Mark Wiskow & Susan Strommer.* Left to right: $30, $50+, $50, $65

Two 12 and an 18R mixing bowl from the 1920s, early to mid-1930s, and late 1930s-early 1940s. The early and middle period bowls measure 8.5" in diameter. The late period bowl measures 9.5" in diameter. *Courtesy of June Sakata Scoggins.* 8.5" d.: $85; 9.5" d.: $95

Early Bristol blue banded mixing bowl (24), the smallest of the line from a nested set, 7" d. *Courtesy of June Sakata Scoggins.* $35

Blended glaze mixing bowls: #9 bowl, 10.5" d.; #12 bowl, 9.5" h.; #18 bowl, 8.25" d.; #24 bowl, 6 7/8" d.; #30 bowl, 6.25" d.; #36 bowl, 5.25" d. Note that the two smallest mixing bowls have no rims while the larger four have rolled rims. *Courtesy of Mark Wiskow & Susan Strommer.* #9: $225; #12: $195; #18: $145; #24: $125; #30: $95; #36: $85

Blended glaze mixing bowls (numbers 9, 12, and 18). Mixing bowl 9, 10" d.; 12: 9" d.; 18: 8" d. *Courtesy of June Sakata Scoggins.* 9: $225; 12: $195; 18: $145

A #18 mixing bowl glazed in black with orange, 8.25" d.; a creamer glazed in blue and red, 3.5" h.; and a straight-sided bowl (possibly a pet feeding bowl) with an unusual glaze blending including white with blue and rust (white was a highly unusual Pacific glaze color), 6.75" d. x 2.25" h. *Courtesy of Mark Wiskow & Susan Strommer.* Mixing bowl: $145; creamer: $95; straight-sided bowl: $225

Five steins (#502), marked with the diamond shaped "Pacific" mark, 4.5" h. The white glazed stein is rare. *Courtesy of Robert R. Perry.* $125+ each

Blended glaze steins. *Courtesy of Mark Wiskow & Susan Strommer.* $165 each

Early green glazed tankard pitcher (#507), 8.5" h.; steins (#502), 4.5" h. The steins are marked with diamond shaped, impressed "Pacific" marks. *Pitcher courtesy of Ken Solus & Larry Holben. Mugs courtesy of Walter Schirra Ceramics (calpottery@mindspring.com).* Pitcher: $295+; mugs: $125+ each

Early Pacific pitcher (#507) and steins (#502), stamped or impressed with the diamond shaped "Pacific" manufacturer's mark. Pitcher: 6.5" h.; steins: 4.5" h. *Courtesy of June Sakata Scoggins.* Pitcher: $295+; steins: $125+ each

Pitchers (#507) and steins (#502). Pitchers: 8.25" and 6.5" h. Steins: 4.5" h. *Courtesy of June Sakata Scoggins.* Pitchers: $295+ each; steins: $125+ each

Additional examples of blended glaze steins. *Courtesy of Naomi's of San Francisco.* $165 each

Blended glaze tankard pitcher (#507) and steins (#502). Pitcher: 8.5" h, steins: 4.5" h. *Courtesy of Mark Wiskow & Susan Strommer.* Pitcher: $450+; steins: $165 each

Early blended glaze tankard pitcher (#507), 8.5" h., and steins (#502) with impressed diamond shaped "Pacific" mark and paper diamond shaped "Pacific Pottery" label. 8.5" h. tankard. *Courtesy of "Jamie" of Star Antiques of San Francisco.* Tankard: $450+; steins: $165 each

Four blended glaze tankard pitchers (#507), 8.5" h. The red blended glaze is very rare. *Courtesy of June Sakata Scoggins.* $450+ each

Various blended glazes on a yellow ware tankard pitcher (#507), 8.5" h., and yellow ware steins (#502), 4.5" h. *Courtesy of June Sakata Scoggins.* Pitcher: $450; steins: $165+ each

A Decade of Colorful Tablewares & Kitchenwares: 1932-1942

Tablewares, kitchenwares, and artwares were produced by a number of California pottery companies to fill the void left when home and office construction largely ceased with the onset of fiscal hard times, beginning with the Wall Street Stock Market crash in 1929. Among California's most influential firms to enter the domestic and artwares market with popular, mass produced ceramics were the J.A. Bauer Pottery Company, Pacific Clay Products, Gladding, McBean & Company, Metlox, and Vernon Kilns. Bauer Pottery began a Depression era craze for solid colored, durable, mix-and-match dinner and kitchenwares with "California Colored Pottery." Pacific Clay Products was following closely on Bauer's heels, presenting their own take on mix-and-match dining and colorful artwares in 1932. Both companies encouraged hostesses to be adventurous with their table settings. They advised homemakers to "mix-and-match" different pieces in different solid glaze colors to produce a varied, colorful effect at the dinner table not previously possible with wares featuring more standard decorative motifs.

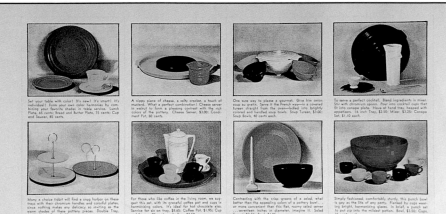

This is a Pacific advertising folder. Front left reads: "Informal! Color for your table. Pacific Pottery." Top left image: "Small accents of color for a conventional table, or valued members of the dinner service by Pacific. Squat, circular and pleasing, these small pieces lend charm to modern design. Sugar and Creamer Set, $1.20; Salt and Pepper Set, $1.50." Bottom left image: "Candies, nuts and even relishes are perfectly at home in this comely little dish with its dainty fluted edges. An occasional dish that is always welcome and it's nice to have several in different colors . . . $1.75 each." This folder also advertises one of Pacific Pottery's merchants, "Exclusively featured by Hollywood Potteries at Balboa Park San Diego, Calif." *Courtesy of Bill Harmon, Nine Lives Antiques.*

Inside the folder the captions beneath the images read as follows. **Top row, left to right:** "Set your table with color! It's new! It's smart! It's individual! Form your own color harmonies by combining your favorite shades in table service. Lunch Plate, 65 cents; Bread and Butter Plate, 35 cents; Cup and Saucer, 85 cents." "A nippy piece of chese, a salty cracker, a touch of mustard. What a perfect combination! Cheese server in walnut to form a pleasing contrast with the rich colors o fthe pottery. Cheese Server, $3.00; Condiment Pot, 60 cents." "One sure way to please a gourmet. Give him onion soup au gratin. Serve it the French way—in a covered tureen straight from the oven—ladled into brightly colored and handled soup bowls. Soup Tureen, $3.00; Soup Bowls, 40 cents each." "To serve a perfect cocktail. Blend ingredients in mixer. Stir with chromium spoon. Pour into cocktail cups that fit into canape plate. Have at hand tray, heaped with appetizers. 16 inch Tray, $2.50; Mixer, $3.25; Canape Set, $1.10 each." **Bottom row, left to right:** "Many a choice tidbit will find a snug harbor on these trays with their chromium handles and colorful plates, since nothing makes any delicacy so inviting as the warm shades of these pottery pieces. Double Tray, $1.75; Single Tray, $1.25." "For those who like coffee in the living room, we suggest this set, with its graceful coffee pot and cups in harmonizing colors. It's ideal for hot chocolate also. Service for six on tray, $8.65; Coffee Pot, $1.95; Cup and Saucer, 70 cents each; Tray, $2.50." "Contrasting with the crisp greens of a salad, what better than the appealing colors of a pottery bowl . . . or more convenient than this flat, roomy salad server . . . seventeen inches in diameter, imagine it. Salad Server, $3.50; Bowl, $1.95." "Simply fashioned, comfortably sturdy, this punch bowl is gay as the life of any party. Flanked by cups wearing bright, harmonizing glazes. In brief, a punch set to put zip into the mildest potion. Bowl, $3.50; Cups, 35 cents each." *Courtesy of Bill Harmon, Nine Lives Antiques.*

Hostess Ware, newer 1940s era (c. 1941-1942 war effort wares) 600 line, including a diamond shaped stamped "Hostess Ware" (at the top of the diamond) mark. Large plate (#678), 10 3/8" d.; yellow plate (#614), 6.5" d.; large green bowl (#677), 8 3/8" d.; red bowl (no number), 5.5" d.; teacup (#608) and saucer (#609); and coffee cup (#634) and saucer. *Courtesy of June Sakata Scoggins.* #678 plate: $24; #614 plate: $10; #677 bowl: $95; red bowl: $45; teacup and saucer: $22 set; coffee cup and saucer: $45 set

Pie plate and bakers were offered with removable wooden and metal handles that fitted into the slots molded into the body of the ware. Pie plate (#638), 10" d.; baker (#224), 8" d.; and baker (#223), 8.5" d. *Courtesy of June Sakata Scoggins.* $85 each

When Pacific designed and produced its colorful pottery for the home, three factors helped to guide the design department in specific directions. First among them was the aforementioned economic depression. With money tight, homeowners cast off the expensive formal dinners of their parents' and grandparents' generations in favor of informal, buffet style dining. Consumers sought pottery that was inexpensive yet presentable and durable. The glaze colors preferred were bright and uplifting during hard times.

With money tight, Pacific and other pottery manufacturers were looking for simpler forms, fewer pieces in sets, and simpler decorations to keep costs down. The streamlining of Art Deco worked well, eliminating fancy ornamentation. The trend toward informal dining allowed for the elimination of many incidental table items that had been so popular in decades past (bone dishes, cup plates, and on and on). The simple, brightly colored glazes eliminated the need for expensive, elaborate designs created and applied by skilled artisans. For Pacific, this quickly culminated in the production of their best known line, Hostess Ware, which embodied all of these features.

The second factor influencing design was the repeal of Prohibition in 1933. Repeal was said to have helped do away with formal dinner parties as well. With the free flow of alcohol came the demand for informal, colorful tablewares to set the mood for a lively, relaxed evening. One might suppose that durability of the ware was a plus here as well, particularly if the night became very lively indeed!

Martini pitcher (very rare) in Delphinium blue, 10.5" h.; cocktail cups (#651) in cobalt, yellow, green, orange, and Delphinium. All are resting on a handled target plate in Delph, 15" d. *Courtesy of Mark Wiskow & Susan Strommer.* Cocktail cups: $95+ each; target plate: $195+

Finally, women's fashions influenced glaze coloration. During the 1930s, women began to wear clothing in soft pastel shades. Once these pastel colors were accepted in clothing, the same colors in ceramics and other home furnishings soon followed. By the 1940s, even Hollywood cowboys were discarding their standard black and white hats in favor of pastel shades!

By 1935, the trend in the pottery market was described in the trade journals as follows,

"Demand for dinnerware was marked by interest in small sets, including services for 4 and 6 persons, and for 36 and 48 piece sets to retail at $5 to $8. Kitchen crockery and breakfast sets were ordered in large quantities in practically all price ranges. The demand in kitchen ware was for colors, with red, green, and blue preferred. Producers who experimented with red decorations for kitchenware this season are featuring the color in new lines. The red, trimmed with ivory, is shown in enamelware, kitchen tools and other items.

All lines of American-made dinner sets were in demand for the special promotions at the beginning of the new year. Retailers are becoming strong in their advocacy of domestic production of chinaware on a wide scale. One large department store merchandiser said that in his opinion price had been an overworked appeal. He is now among those in favor of the development of a home pottery industry and style trends to end price competition. With the exceptionally fine designers whom domestic potters have enrolled there is every incentive now to carry on a style competition for the domestic trade." (*Ceramic Industry* 1935)

Advertisement in *House Beautiful* magazine in October 1936. The desired colorful look for that kitchen of 1936, featuring brightly colored pottery and other wares. *Courtesy of Bill Harmon, Nine Lives Antiques.*

By 1935, an interesting new outlet for both ceramics and glassware had presented itself. Movie theater chains began ordering low priced wares to give away to movie patrons, luring audiences into their seats. Over the course of a year, 52-piece china sets were given away, one piece and one week at a time. This was an opportunity for pottery firms to produce inexpensive (and probably unmarked) items that fattened their balance sheets.

In 1937, California potteries would produce roughly two million dollars worth of colorful tablewares. Pacific Clay Products manufactured a significant portion of that pottery themselves. Of their product, the California pottery industry was proud to point out that theirs was high quality merchandise, merchandise to be found in art and department stores . . . not in low-priced shops! That last bit was a dig at their competitors in Ohio, many of whom sold to the chains and other discount stores.

A full page advertisement by Pacific Pottery that appeared in *House Beautiful* magazine in October 1936. It reads: "Clever hostesses everywhere choose Pacific. [Top, center] New York: New Yorkers seem to prefer their pottery decorated. We've pictured only one of many, many smart designs and color combinations offered in Pacific's new "starter" set. You'll find that the mellow textures and soft, glowing tones of a pottery service are as practical as they are pleasing. In any of the eight Pacific colors and a wide variety of designs. Set includes twenty-three pieces, service for four. Complete: $12.75. [Top, right] Los Angeles: Californians liked the combination of crisp salads and bright pottery so well that they demanded other pieces to harmonize. Plates were added to the bowls, then cups and saucers. Expert designers and ceramic craftsmen were employed, and now there are pottery pieces for every serving need. Decorated salad set (sketched above) includes matching bowl, lacquered wooden fork and spoon, six salad plates. Complete: $5.75. [Center, left] Boston: An exiled New Englander, remembering his native Massachusetts, designed this two-piece tribute to the immortal baked bean. The wide-mouthed bean pot makes the beans juicier, the inevitable washing easier, and the sixteen-inch tray for brown bread makes the service complete. Ideal for buffet service. Set: $3.50. [Center, center] Honolulu: Hawaii likes Pacific's fruit and flower bowls and vases, with their soft finishes in ivory, pastel green, and blue. Our favorite is the three-piece lily console set that is illustrated above. Bowl: $3.00; pair of candlesticks: $3.00. Note: Hawaii also likes Pacific's colorful tableware. [Center, right] New Orleans: The set shown above is recommended highly for Coffee Royals by the very best authorities on the subject, but even if you take your coffee straight, you'll find it has a much more soothing flavor when served in gaily-colored pottery. Coffee jug: $1.50; sixteen-inch tray: $2.50; cup and saucer: 65 c. [Bottom, left] Chicago: Here's a plate with a two-way stretch. Used with a plank it's a perfect steak plate . . . with the individual fitted baker, it becomes an attractive service for any baked entree. Serv-all plate: 85c; baker: 25c; plank: 70c. [Bottom, center] San Francisco: For lovers of the flowing bowl, Pacific presents a festive Tom and Jerry set. Gallon-sized bowl, polished aluminum ladle, six mugs. Set complete: $6.50. [Bottom, right] There are eight beautiful colors to choose from when you buy Pacific pottery. Every piece is individually inspected and carries a money-back guarantee against imperfections. Look for the diamond-shaped label for pottery that is dependable as well as decorative. Prices Slightly Lower West of the Rockies. Phone to Find Who Sells It See Last Page. Pacific Pottery from California. Made by pottery division, Pacific Clay Products, Los Angeles, California." *Courtesy of Bill Harmon, Nine Lives Antiques.*

Wares for the Table and the Kitchen

In 1932, Pacific jumped into both the domestic pottery and artwares markets with attractive, heavy, brightly glazed ceramics with predominantly single glaze colors. Very quickly, their Hostess Ware line began to rival the wares Bauer first presented in 1930. In time, the Hostess Ware line would have a greater diversity of wares than Bauer and would give its competitor a run for the money. Early glaze colors included red, yellow, blue, and green under imaginative names such as Apache Red, Royal Blue (cobalt), Silver Green, and Canary Yellow. Later Apricot, White (Sierra White), Turquoise, and Delphinium Blue were added to the mix. However, if those colors did not satisfy, special order glaze colors were also available for a price, Black and White among them. Glaze colors and names would change over times and other colors would be added.

Cheese board (#635), tray (#616), covered divided dish (#640—unmarked) and sugar and creamer (#403 & #404). Tray 12" l.; divided dish, 12" l. *Courtesy of Robert R. Perry.* Cheese board: $165; tray: $125; covered divided dish with lid: $145; sugar & creamer set without lid: $55

Pacific Pottery advertisement from the *House and Garden* magazine, April 1935. It reads: "From Colorful California. Vivid, Arresting Pottery in Smart Dinner and Buffet Services. In the rich, warm colors reminiscent of old Spain . . . yet styled to the modern mood . . . Pacific pottery brings the *fiesta* spirit to present day dining.

Whether it appears as the first cheerful note on the breakfast tray . . . as part of the color harmony of an informal lunch . . . a zestful background for buffet suppers . . . or even as a gala touch to more formal dinners . . . there's a subtle magic about these decorative pieces.

Pacific pottery is satin-smooth in texture. Heat and cold resistant. Designed for every serving need, at prices surprisingly moderate. Six appealing colors, Apache Red, Lemon Yellow, Delphinium Blue, Jade Green, Sierra White, Pacific Blue. Sold at leading stores . . . Descriptive folder in colors available upon request. Pacific Pottery Division of Pacific Clay Products, Los Angeles, California." *Courtesy of Bill Harmon, Nine Lives Antiques.*

Eight cup teapot (#440) and 11 oz. tumblers (#409), one with an impressed "Pacific" mark, number "409," and a paper label. Teapot: 5.5" h. x 11" l. Tumblers: 5" h. *Courtesy of June Sakata Scoggins.* Teapot: $195; tumblers: $55 each

Black Hostess Ware dinner plate, 11" d., and a full sized sugar bowl with lid. This black glaze color is extremely rare. *Courtesy of Mark Wiskow & Susan Strommer.* Plate: $75+; sugar bowl: $125+

Pacific Hostess Wares decorated all in white are rare. All white place setting: demi cup and saucer (#689); individual coffee pot (#443), 6.25" h.; dinner plate (#613), 11.5" d.;. salad plate (#610), 7.5" d.; lug or onion soup (#37), 5.75" d, 6.25" handle to handle; footed goblet (#433), 5.25" h.; tumbler (#422), 4.25" h.; old style egg cup (#642), 3.75" h.; and a pedestal base sherbet (#654), 3" h. *Courtesy of Mark Wiskow & Susan Strommer.* Demi cup & saucer: $85 set; coffee pot: $295+; dinner plate: $32; salad plate: $25+; onion soup: $85; goblet: $165; tumbler: $30+; egg cup: $85+; and sherbet: $85

Rare all white serving pieces: after dinner six cup coffee pot (#442), 9.25" h.; gravy boat (#641), 8.5" l; and punch/salad bowl (#311), 11" d. *Courtesy of Mark Wiskow & Susan Strommer.* Coffee pot: $295+; gravy boat: $70; punch/salad bowl: $165+

By 1935, the ceramics trade journals reported that Pacific was capitalizing on a combination of pastel glazes and a strong stoneware body material. That year, the trade journals also addressed Pacific's introduction of Decorated wares, stating that, "Contrasting colors and designs glazed onto the ware are offered in a number of styles and have gained wide attention due to the softness of the color effects." (*Ceramic Industry* 1935, p. 72) Further, the article mentioned that Pacific maintained a special design department for consumers wishing to have exclusive decorated wares made for them. Decorated wares featured patterns and scenes applied by hand over the base glaze colors on Hostess Ware bodies.

By 1937, consumers were looking for thinner, more delicate wares. Pacific responded first with the introduction of the Coralitos line, followed shortly thereafter by the Arcadia line. Later lines also included decal decorations. As World War II loomed on the horizon in 1941, Pacific added a variety of hand painted lines, then becoming popular, to their offerings. Among these late offerings were the Grape, Strawberry, Hibiscus, French Ivy, and Shasta Daisy lines.

Now, let's look at each of these areas in more detail.

Coralitas after dinner coffee pot marked "Pacific Made In USA X39," 9" h. *Courtesy of Walter Schirra Ceramics (calpottery@mindspring.com).* $85

Molded and painted California Grape pattern pitcher, teapot, and covered sugar. Pitcher, 10.25" h. *Courtesy of June Sakata Scoggins.* Pitcher: $95; teapot: $125; covered sugar: $45

Hostess Ware

As the company transitioned from the production of their earlier utilitarian wares, artwares, and serving pieces to the table, kitchen, and artwares of the 1930s, early plain ware pieces were introduced into the market. As with the J. A. Bauer Company, plain wares were to be the forerunners of the eminently successful Hostess Ware line. These items have many of the forms of Hostess Ware without the addition of the distinctive molded ring motifs Hostess Wares are known for. No transition occurs overnight. At times, plain wares feature the blended glazes developed in the 1920s.

Plain ware low curved edge coupe salads: smallest to largest: #663, circular Pacific mark, 12.25" d.; #624, unmarked, 15.25" d.; #623, 18" d. *Courtesy of June Sakata Scoggins.* #663: $125; #624: $175; #623: $225

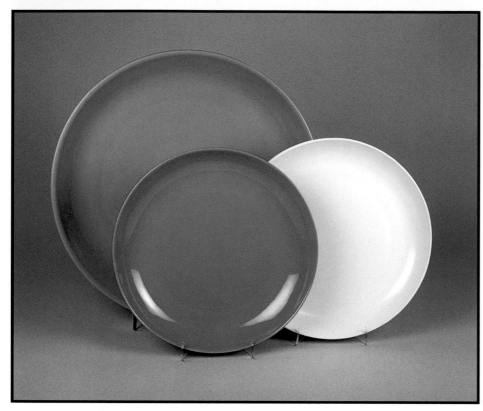

Plain ware low coupe salads: two #663 bowls and one #624, 15.25" d. All are unmarked. These coupe salads would be used in the Hostess Ware line. *Courtesy of June Sakata Scoggins.* #663: $125 each; #624: $175

Top right: Early plain ware in yellow. Both the server and the tray measure 17.5" in diameter. The mixing bowl measures 9.25" in diameter. *Courtesy of June Sakata Scoggins.* Server and tray: $135+ each; mixing bowl: $95

Bottom right: Two early low tab handled shirred egg dishes, unmarked, 6.5" d. x 8.25" across the tabs. *Courtesy of June Sakata Scoggins.* $75 each

Plain ware batter bowl and mixing bowl in cobalt. Batter bowl: 12" handle to spout x 4" h. Mixing bowl: 8" d. Both are unmarked. *Courtesy of Walter Schirra Ceramics (calpottery@mindspring.com).* Left to right: $175, $85

Early small mixing bowl (#36) with a stamped diamond shaped "Pacific" mark. This is an interesting late plain ware piece that was glazed in the later Hostess Ware Apache Red glazing. 5.25" d. *Courtesy of June Sakata Scoggins.* $45

Plain ware utility ware/kitchenware: large black batter bowl (black is a rare Pacific glaze color), 9.25" d. x 4 7/8" h.; small cobalt batter bowl, 8" d. x 4" h.; mixing bowl in orange, 6.25" d.; and a mixing bowl in green, 5.25" d. *Courtesy of Mark Wiskow & Susan Strommer.* Black batter bowl: $400+; cobalt batter bowl: $165; orange mixing bowl: $95; green mixing bowl: $85

Early plain ware custard cup, unmarked, and Hostess Ware custard cup, marked "Pacific Made In USA 206." Each cup measures 3.75" in diameter. *Courtesy of Naomi's of San Francisco.* $20 each

Cobalt plain ware mixing bowl (#9), 10.25" d.; unmarked. plain ware bean pot with lid (sits in the center of a platter with a rise in it or a ball jug with tumblers), 6.5" h.; plain ware tab handled shirred egg dish (#216), 11" w. across tabs. *Courtesy of Walter Schirra Ceramics (calpottery@mindspring.com).* Left to right: $125, $95, $95+

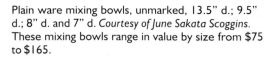

Plain ware mixing bowls, unmarked, 13.5" d.; 9.5" d.; 8" d. and 7" d. *Courtesy of June Sakata Scoggins.* These mixing bowls range in value by size from $75 to $165.

Plain ware cobalt covered water server, 6.5" h.; pitcher, 4" h. to spout; large ball tumbler, 5.5" h. All are unmarked. *Courtesy of Walter Schirra Ceramics (calpottery@mindspring.com).* Left to right: $125, $45, $95

Early plain ware bean pot (lidded and one handled), and two sizes of pitchers. Bean pot: 5.75" h.; pitchers: 4.75" and 3" h. One piece was marked with a printed black diamond shaped "Pacific" manufacturer's mark, the others are unmarked. *Courtesy of June Sakata Scoggins.* Bean pot: $95+; 4.75" h. pitcher: $35+; 3" h. pitcher: $25+

Before Hostess Ware used these, the ball jug and ball tumblers were "plain ware:" utility ware ball pitcher (#420), 9" h.; two large ball tumblers in cobalt and orange, 5.5" h.; and two small 9 oz. ball tumblers (#419) in white and blended green and red, 4.75" h. *Courtesy of Mark Wiskow & Susan Strommer.* Ball jug: $125; large ball tumblers: $95 each; small white ball tumbler: $55+; blended green and red small ball tumbler: $95+

Plain ware circular cake plate (#619), 14" d.; plain ware ball jug and ball tumblers, jug 9" h, 9 oz. tumblers 5" h. All of these items are in glazed in cobalt and all are un-marked. *Courtesy of Walter Schirra Ceramics (calpottery@mindspring.com).* Jug: $125; tumblers: $55+ each

A large and popular line, Hostess Ware was produced from the early 1930s on through Pacific's tableware producing years. Hostess Ware (the name appears in advertisements and catalogs as either two words or the single word Hostessware; take your choice) encompassed a wide variety of wares including tablewares, serving dishes, kitchenwares, and tea and coffee services. The body shapes were in tune with Depression era Art Deco styling and the glazes ranged over time from bright colors to pastels. In 1935, Hostess Ware was available in six glaze colors: Delphinium Blue, Royal Blue, Silver Green, Apache Red, Sierra White, and Canary Yellow. In 1936, Hostess Ware expanded its glaze color offerings to eight, including Apricot, Delphinium Blue, Royal Blue, Turquoise Blue, Silver Green, Apache Red, Sierra White, and Canary Yellow. By 1937, with this range of colors in place, Pacific would advise, "Restrain yourself to two harmonizing shades for your informal table, or let yourself go in a mad riot of ALL the colors." (*American Home*, 1937)

Red Hostess Ware place setting. Plate, incised mark "Pacific 613," 12.75" d.; plate, 11" d.; plate, incised mark "Pacific 611," 9" d.; plate, incised mark "Pacific 610," 7.25" d.; smallest plate unmarked, 6.25" d. *Courtesy of Robert R. Perry.* $10 to $125+ each depending on the piece.

Early plain ware: 9 oz. ball tumblers (#419), 5" h.; 3 qt. ball jug (#420), 9" h.; and tray (#452), 16" d. *Courtesy of Robert R. Perry.* Tumblers: $55+ each; jug: $125; tray: $150

Cobalt circular cake plate and plates: left to right, cake plate, marked "Pacific Made In USA 619" (molded raised); plate, incised mark "Pacific 613,"12.75" d.; plate, 11" d.; plate, incised mark "Pacific 611," 9" d.; plate, incised mark "Pacific 610," 7.25" d.; smallest plate unmarked, 6.25" d. *Courtesy of Walter Schirra Ceramics (calpottery@mindspring.com)*. Cake plate: $195+; 11" d. plate: $24+; 9" d. plate: $24; 7.25" d. plate: $18; 6.25" d. plate: $10

Light blue Hostess Ware place setting. *Courtesy of Robert R. Perry*. $10 to $125+ each depending on the piece.

Green place setting. *Courtesy of Robert R. Perry*. $10 to $125+ each depending on the piece.

Apricot place setting. *Courtesy of Robert R. Perry*. $10 to $125+ each depending on the piece.

Aqua place setting: dinner (#613), luncheon (#607), & bread and butter (#614) plates, bowl (#36R), sauce dish (#601), custard cup (#206), and cup (#608) and saucer (#609). *Courtesy of Robert R. Perry.* $10 to $125+ each depending on the piece.

Lavender plate (#614), a rare glaze color, 6.25" d. *Courtesy of Robert R. Perry.* $30+

Hostess Ware 1930s era two tiered tidbit tray featuring 11" and 7.5" d. plates; large six cup teapot, 7" h.; and low four cup teapot, 4" h. *Courtesy of June Sakata Scoggins.* Tidbit: $45; teapots: $195 each

Hostess Ware cobalt low bowls: sauce dish, marked "606 Pacific," 6" d.; sauce dish, marked "601 Pacific," 5.5" d.; coaster, marked "Pacific Made In USA 432," 4" d.; and an unmarked butter chip (#207), 3.25" d. *Courtesy of Walter Schirra Ceramics (calpottery@mindspring.com).* Left to right: $30, $30, $35, $45

Back: grill plates (#615), 11" d. Front: relish dishes (#603), 9.5" d. The left hand relish dish is a later model featuring a circular mark. *Courtesy of Naomi's of San Francisco.* Grill plates: $65+ each; relish dishes: $75 each

Grill plate (#615), unmarked, 11" d.; divided relish dish, marked "Pacific 603;" gravy boat, marked "Pacific Made In USA 641," 8.5" l. *Courtesy of Walter Schirra Ceramics (calpottery@mindspring.com).* Grill plate: $65+; celery/olive dish: $75+; gravy boat: $55

Back row: three part relish dishes (#603) in orange, light blue, and yellow, 9.25" d. Center: center handle four part relish dish (#662), orange, 9 3/8" d. Two salad dressing servers (#665) featuring two compartments and tab handles in light blue and orange surround the center handle relish dish, 6" l. (8.5" handle to handle). Individual salad dressing boats (#666) in cobalt, yellow, apricot, light blue and orange, 7.25" l. x 1.25" h. *Courtesy of Mark Wiskow & Susan Strommer.* #603 relish dishes: $75+ each; #662 relish dish: $95; #665 servers: $65+ each; #666 boats: $45+ each

Grill plates: note that the largest grill plate has a small triangular tab along the inside rim of the plate to keep the plates from wobbling when stacked. The smaller plates (#615) lack this feature. Large white grill plate: 12" d.; small grill plate: 11" d. *Courtesy of June Sakata Scoggins.* 12" d.: $85+; 11" d.: $65 each

Four compartment relish dish with a central wooden handle (#662), 9.5" d. *Courtesy of June Sakata Scoggins.* $95

"Serve-All Dinner Plate" marked "Pacific Made In USA 661," 11.25" d. Used in conjunction with other pieces, this serve-all dinner plate becomes a serving tray. *Courtesy of Naomi's of San Francisco.* $95

Chip 'n Dip set with #661 serve-alls and #205 baker without a lid. *Courtesy of Robert R. Perry.* Tray: $95+; baker: $25+

Chip 'n Dip sets: two serve-all trays (#661) and lidded bakers (#205), 11.25" d. tray, 5" across tabs for bakers. *Courtesy of June Sakata Scoggins.* Tray: $95; baker with lid: $45

Bean pots ranging from 6.5 to 6" h. Large serving tray (#452—listed in Pacific catalogs as only for the Sunday Supper Set). Small serve-all tray (#661), with a circular "Pacific Made In USA" mark. The small red bean pot is an early example and has no mark. *Courtesy of Robert R. Perry.* Bean pots: $95+ each; #452 tray: $150+; #661 tray: $95+

Cobalt circular tab handled tray, marked with an incised catalog number "413" and five stilt marks. 15" d. *Courtesy of Walter Schirra Ceramics (calpottery@mindspring.com).* $195

"Sunday Supper Set." Tray (#452), large bean pot (#232), individual casseroles or bakers (#205), all are either marked with circular "Pacific Made In USA" mark or unmarked. Tray, 16" d. *Courtesy of Robert R. Perry.* Tray: $150+; bean pot: $95+; casseroles/bakers: $45 each with lid

Target tray (#451), unmarked, 16" d.; cheese board with wooden cutting board (#635), 11" d. *Courtesy of Walter Schirra Ceramics (calpottery@mindspring.com).* Tray: $195; cheese dish: $165

Cheese boards (#635): red, 11.25" d.; green: 11 1/8" d. *Courtesy of June Sakata Scoggins.* $165 each

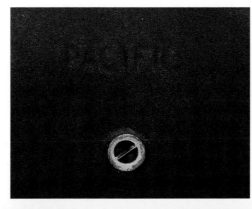

Low rectangular tray (#1063), marked with a molded "Pacific Made In USA" mark, 7.5" l. This is a very unusual piece. *Courtesy of Bill Stern (wbstern@aol.com).* $200

Three Hostess Ware cheese boards (#635), marked "Pacific 613" (#613 is the designation for a Hostess Ware dinner plate—from which the cheese boards are made), 11" d.; two candy dishes marked "633," 9.5" l. *Courtesy of Naomi's of San Francisco.* Cheese boards: $165 each; candy dishes: $65 each

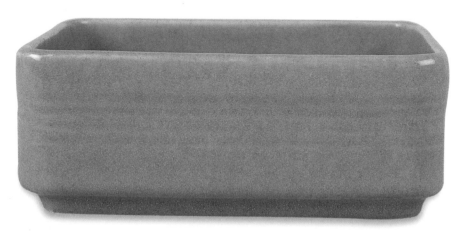

Three rectangular platters: orange platter (#617), 15" w.; green platter (#616), 12.5" w.; 10.5" orange toast platter (#659), 10.5" w. *Courtesy of Mark Wiskow & Susan Strommer.* Left to right: $175, $125, $95

This piece is listed twice in the company's price listings as either a cigarette box or a refrigerator box (#426). In either case, it would need a lid. This item measures 3.5" x 4.5". The refrigerator box was listed as measuring 3.5" only. *Courtesy of Bill Stern (wbstern@aol.com).* $200+ with a lid

Four fish platters, all marked "Pacific Made In USA 660." 15.75" l. each. *Courtesy of Walter Schirra Ceramics (calpottery@mindspring.com); Courtesy of Naomi's of San Francisco.* $195+ each

Pacific tray, marked "Pacific 444," 14" l.; divided vegetable bowl (#640), unmarked, 12" l.; oval bowl, marked "Pacific 644," 9.25" l. *Courtesy of Naomi's of San Francisco.* Tray: $125; divided bowl: $95; oval bowl: $85

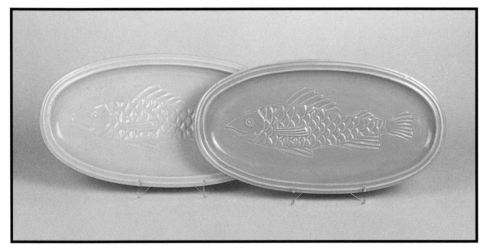

Two fish platters (#660) in yellow and green, 15.75" l. *Courtesy of Mark Wiskow & Susan Strommer.* $195+

Oval trays and bowls, including a lidded bowl: large oval bowl (#664), 12" l.; small oval bowls (#644), 9.25" l.; oval trays (#444), 14" l. These oval trays and bowls include both a circular manufacturer's mark and an earlier impressed "Pacific" mark with catalog numbers. *Courtesy of June Sakata Scoggins.* #664 bowl with lid: $145; #664 bowl without lid: $95; #644 bowl: $85; #444 tray: $125

A variety of Hostess Ware pieces. Top: four footed low salad bowl, 12.75" d. Center: orange soup bowl with tab handles and cover, 7" l. tab to tab, 4" h. to finial. Bottom: Two low four footed bowl in cobalt (#315) and turquoise (#314), 8" d. and 8.25" d.; and an orange covered rectangular butter dish (#669), 6 1/8" l. tab to tab; 2.5" h. *Courtesy of Mark Wiskow & Susan Strommer.* Top: $125; center: $75+; bottom: bowls: $65 each; butter dish: $200+

Cobalt covered casserole, marked "Pacific Made In USA, 209," 8.5" d. x 5" h.; oval divided dish (#640), unmarked, 12" l.; and small detachable handled pie plate, marked "Pacific 645," 8" d. *Courtesy of Walter Schirra Ceramics (calpottery@mindspring.com).* Casserole: $125+; divided dish: $95+; pie plate: $85

Cobalt bowls: four footed salad bowl (#315), unmarked, 8" d.; tab handled onion soup bowl (#37—soup/cereal bowl), unmarked, 6" d.; unmarked bowl, 5.5" d.; deep mush bowl, incised mark "36R Pacific," 5.25" d. *Courtesy of Walter Schirra Ceramics (calpottery@mindspring.com).* Left to right: $65+, $45+, $45+, $45+

Top, left to right: Two compartment salad dressing server (#665), 8.5" across the tab handles; sauce dish (#606), 6.25" d.; sauce dish (#601), 5.75" d.
Bottom, left to right: onion soup (#37), tab handled, 6.5" across the tabs; deep mush bowl (36R), 5.5" d.; custard cup (#206); and individual salad dressing boat (#666), 7.5" l. *Courtesy of June Sakata Scoggins.* #665 server: $65; #606 sauce dish: $45; #601 sauce dish: $45; #75 onion soup: $65; #36R mush bowl: $45; #206 custard cup: $20+; #666 individual salad dressing boats: $45+

Unusual forms in Hostess Ware. Large and small bowls with the same decoration, large: #677, 8.5" d. to rim; small soup/cereal (no number) but with a diamond shaped stamped black "Pacific" mark, 5.5" d.; covered baker (#205), 5" across tabs; individual vegetable (#667), 6.25" l. *Courtesy of June Sakata Scoggins.* #677 bowl: $95; soup/cereal bowl: $45; baker: $45; vegetable bowl: $55

Three sizes of Hostess Ware salad bowls. The largest is a low salad bowl bearing a "314" impressed mark and measures 12.5" in diameter. The medium sized bowl (the green #310 bowl above the #314 yellow bowl) is unmarked, measuring 9" in diameter. The smallest bowls (#315) measure 8" in diameter. These small bowls carry an impressed "Pacific" mark with a number or a circular "Pacific Made In USA" mark with the "315" number in the center. The light blue bowl on the top of the stack is a #315, carries a circular mark, and measures 8.25" in diameter. *Courtesy of Robert R. Perry.* #314 bowl: $125+; #310 bowl: $85; #315 bowls: $65+ each

Hostess Ware cobalt pudding dish (#214), 8.5" d.; cobalt pudding dish (#213), 7.5" d. *Courtesy of Walter Schirra Ceramics (calpottery@mindspring.com).* Left to right: $65, $55

Hostess Ware four footed punch and salad bowls, (#312) 14", (#311) 11.25" and (#311) 11" d. *Courtesy of Robert R. Perry.* Left to right: $350+, $145+, $145+

Cobalt Hostess Ware four footed bowls: salad/punch bowl (#312), 14" d.; low salad bowl (#314) 13" d.; and salad bowl (#310), 9" d. All of these bowls are unmarked. *Courtesy of Walter Schirra Ceramics (calpottery@mindspring.com).* Left to right: $350, $125, $85+

Hostess Ware low salad bowls. Back: low salad bowls (#314), marked "314" only, 12.25" d.; front: low salad bowl (#315), 8" d. *Courtesy of Dennis Canavan.* Back: $125+ each; front: $65

Hostess Ware bowls marked with a late ink stamped black diamond shaped "Hostess Ware" mark. 5.5" d. *Courtesy of June Sakata Scoggins.* $45+ each

Rare all white Hostess Ware pieces: mixing bowl (#12), 9.5" d.; deep mush bowl (36R), 5.25" d.; and a ball tumbler (#419), 9 oz., 4 7/8" h. *Courtesy of Mark Wiskow & Susan Strommer.* Mixing bowl: $250+; mush bowl: $60+; tumbler/vase: $70+

Soup tureen (#604) with a slotted lid and an early, small bowl (#36) with an unusual ring design. The tureen is unmarked while the early bowl is marked with an impressed "Pacific" manufacturer's mark and the number. Soup tureen: 10.75" across tabs; small bowl: 5.25" d. *Courtesy of June Sakata Scoggins.* Tureen: $245+; bowl: $85+

Punch bowl (#311), unmarked, 11" d. x 5" h. *Courtesy of June Sakata Scoggins.* $125

Lidded Hostess Wares: cookie jar or pretzel jar (very hard to find, especially with the lid), 9.5" h.; scarce round cobalt casserole (#209) with two rings, a vented lid, and a Pacific label, 8.75" w. x 5" h.; four footed soup tureen (#604—very scarce), 10.75" handle to handle x 5 5/8" h. *Courtesy of Mark Wiskow & Susan Strommer.* Cookie/pretzel jar: $395; casserole: $125; soup tureen: $245

Two covered casseroles (#209), one with a metal frame (#1214). Circular mark. 9" d. *Courtesy of Robert R. Perry.* Casseroles: $125 each; frame for #209 casserole: $20

Yellow roaster (#221) with slots for the insertion of large wooden handles, 18" l. x 7.5" h. to lid handle. This is a rare piece that was originally made and distributed with large wooden handles. *Courtesy of Mark Wiskow & Susan Strommer.* $325+

Cobalt casserole (#200) with a trivet lid (#201). 8" across tab handles. The lid becomes a trivet when the host or hostess is ready to serve. *Courtesy of Mark Wiskow & Susan Strommer.* $150+

Four baking dishes (#222) with detachable wood and metal handles, 6" d. *Courtesy of Mark Wiskow & Susan Strommer.* $55+ each

Three batter bowls (#301), unmarked. The top two bowls measure 4.5" high to the spout and the bottom bowl measures 4" high to the spout. *Courtesy of June Sakata Scoggins.* $150+ each

Custard cups (#206) in front of a tray marked "616 Pacific." The tray measures 12.5" in length. *Courtesy of Naomi's of San Francisco.* Custard cups: $20 each; tray: $125

Cobalt covered tab handled individual baker, marked "Pacific Made In USA 205," 4.5" d.; custard cup (#206), unmarked, 4" d. *Courtesy of Walter Schirra Ceramics (calpottery@mindspring.com).* $35, $20

Hostess Ware mixing bowl set: 9R, 10.75" d.; 12R, 9.5" d.; 18R, 8.5" d.; unmarked, 7.25" d.; 30R, 6.25" d. The marked examples display either a circular "Pacific Made In USA" mark or the smallest feature just an impressed "Pacific" and "30R" mark. *Courtesy of Robert R. Perry.* $65-125 each depending on size.

Hostess Ware mixing bowl, no mark, 7.5" d. $75+

Hostess Ware mixing bowls, ranging in size from 10.75" to 6.5" d. *Courtesy of June Sakata Scoggins.* These mixing bowls range in value by size from $65 to $125.

Cobalt mixing bowl set in five sizes, 10.5" d., 9.75" d., 8.5" d., 7.5" d., and 6.5" d. The 10.5" d. bowl displays the molded mark "Pacific Made In USA 9R." The 9.75" d. bowl displays the molded mark "Pacific Made In USA 12R." The 8.5" d. bowl displays the molded mark "Pacific Made In USA 18R." Both the 7.5" d. and 6.5" d. bowls are unmarked. *Courtesy of Walter Schirra Ceramics (calpottery@mindspring.com).* These bowls range from $125+ to $65+ depending on size.

Large punch bowl (#312) and punch cups, all unmarked, bowl: 14" d. *Courtesy of Robert R. Perry.* Punch bowl: $350; cups: $20+ each

White punch bowl (#312), 14.25" d.; Tom and Jerry mugs (#618); and a yellow tray (#512), unmarked, 17" d. Circular "Pacific Made In USA" mark used, although mugs are both marked and unmarked. Unmarked mugs are early pieces. White is an unusual glaze color in these mugs. *Courtesy of Robert R. Perry.* Punch bowl: $350+; mugs: $20+ each; tray: $135+

Three sizes of salad and punch bowls (right hand back bowl is glazed in early Apache Red) and five Tom & Jerry mugs. Bowls: #312, 14" d.; #311, 11" d.; and #310, 9" d. *Courtesy of Naomi's of San Francisco.* #312 bowl: $350; #311 bowl: $125; #310 bowl: $95; mugs: $20 each

Cobalt punch cup and Tom and Jerry mug. Punch cup (#313), unmarked, 2.25" h.; Tom & Jerry mug (#618), unmarked, 3" h. *Courtesy of Walter Schirra Ceramics (calpottery@mindspring.com).* $20 each

Punch bowl (#312) and punch cups (#313) with unusual glaze coloration: Punch bowl, 14.25" d.; cups, 3.25" d. *Courtesy of June Sakata Scoggins.* Bowl: $350+; cups: $20+ each

Condiment pot (#306), unmarked, 4.25" h. *Courtesy of Walter Schirra Ceramics (calpottery@mindspring.com).* $175+

Large condiment (#306): this lidded piece goes with the large tray with the central insert. This piece is unmarked. 5.75" h. x 8.5" across the handles. *Courtesy of June Sakata Scoggins.* $175+

Early pieces, left to right: condiment jar (#306) and a small marmalade / condiment (#306), 5" and 4" h. *Courtesy of June Sakata Scoggins.* Left to right: $175+ each

Two condiment containers (very rare). The container on the left was made from a small sugar (#307) and a slotted lid, is unmarked, and measures 2.75" high. The larger container on the right is marked with an incised "306" and measures 4" high. *Courtesy of Jerry Kunz. Courtesy of Naomi's of San Francisco.* Left to right: $145+, $175

Condiment pot / jam pot (#448) with a chromium handle, very unusual. *Courtesy of Robert R. Perry.* $195

Condiment jars (#306) in green with a solid lid and orange with a slotted lid (3.75" h. each) surround a cobalt condiment pot with a metal handle. Note the different condiment jar lid finials. *Courtesy of Mark Wiskow & Susan Strommer.* Condiment jars: $175 each; jam jar: $195+

Cookie/pretzel jar (#305), unmarked, 9.25" h. *Courtesy of Ken Solus & Larry Holben.* $395

Rare cobalt cookie/pretzel jar (#305), unmarked, 9.5" h. *Courtesy of Robert R. Perry.* $395+

Hostess Ware egg cups (#642). In the back row are earlier style egg cups measuring 3 7/8" h. while the front features later style cups measuring 3 3/8" h. The earlier style egg cups are glazed in dark blue, light blue, yellow, green, and white. The later style egg cups are glazed in light blue, dark blue, orange, green, and apricot. *Courtesy of Mark Wiskow & Susan Strommer.* $65+ each

Two versions of egg cups and a sherbet in cobalt blue Hostess Ware, all unmarked. Egg cups, 4" h.; sherbet, 3.25" h. *Courtesy of Walter Schirra Ceramics (calpottery@mindspring.com).* $65+ each

Gravy boat (#641), circular "Pacific Made In USA" mark, 8.5" l. *Courtesy of Robert R. Perry.* $55+

Two waffle or covered muffin warmers on ringed plates with wells (#639), 11.25" d. Lids: 9 5/8" d. x 3.5" h. A matched set in light blue and a mixed set with an orange plate and yellow lid. Note: the lid comes vented or unvented; the yellow lid is vented. *Courtesy of Mark Wiskow & Susan Strommer.* Matched set: $285

Cobalt covered muffin/waffle warmer (#639) with domed lid and vent, 11.5" d. *Courtesy of Walter Schirra Ceramics (calpottery@mindspring.com). $285+*

Rare toast cover (#668) with a 7" d. underplate (#610) and a covered butter (#669). *Courtesy of Robert R. Perry. Toast cover and underplate: $165 set; covered butter: $200+*

Waffle warmer (#639) with domed lid and vent glazed in Apricot, 11.5" d. Rare. *Courtesy of Robert R. Perry. $285+*

Cobalt butter dish marked "Pacific Made In USA 669," 6" l. x 2.5" h. *Courtesy of Ken Solus & Larry Holben. $200+*

Cheese and cracker cover (#416—very rare with the cut in rings motif). The lid measures 5.75" h. to the handle. The underplate should be a handled cheese board (#414), 15" d. (although an 11" d. dinner plate is standing in for it in this photograph). The early style cover has the cut in rings while late style covers have raised rings. *Courtesy of Mark Wiskow & Susan Strommer.* $350+

Waffle batter pitcher (#435), syrup pitcher (#435), and covered muffin/waffle dish (#639) in yellow, 7.25", 5.25", 4.25" h. *Courtesy of June Sakata Scoggins.* Left to right: $250, $250, $285

Two waffle batter pitchers (#436— 1 1/2 qt.), 9.5" spout to handle x 7" h. in orange and cobalt and a small syrup pitcher (#435—1 pt.), 9" l. x 5" h. *Courtesy of Mark Wiskow & Susan Strommer.* $250+ each

Yellow long spout syrup pitcher (#435), 4 7/8" h. x 9 1/8" l.; cobalt batter pitcher, 7" h. x 9.5" l.; cobalt condiment pot / jam pot (#448) with chromium handle, 4" h.; and an orange rectangular platter (#617), 15" w. *Courtesy of Mark Wiskow & Susan Strommer.* Syrup pitcher: $250+; batter pitcher: $250+; jam jar: $195+; platter: $175

Syrup pitcher (#435), 1 pt., hand marked "554," 5" h. *Courtesy of Robert R. Perry.* $250

Range salt & pepper shakers and grease jar. It is exceptionally rare to find the grease jar with its lid. 5 1/8" h. grease jar with lid and 4 1/8" h. salt and pepper shakers. In a December 1936 issue of *McCall's*, these sets were said to come in red, blue, green, or yellow and were for the "woman who loves her kitchen." *Courtesy of June Sakata Scoggins.* Three piece set with lid: $295; three piece set without lid: $195

Range salt and peppers (#232), 4" h.; table salt and peppers (#620, #621), 2.25" h. Both are marked but illegible. *Courtesy of Walter Schirra Ceramics (calpottery@mindspring.com).* Range set: $125+; table set: $45+

Range salt and pepper shakers (#232), 4" h. *Courtesy of Naomi's of San Francisco.* $125+ set.

Two range sets (#209): grease jars without lids, 4.75" h.; salt and pepper shakers, 4.25" h. *Courtesy of Robert R. Perry.* Three piece sets without lids: $195+ each

Table salt and pepper shakers (#620, #621), 2.25" h. *Courtesy of Naomi's of San Francisco.* $45+ set

Canapé tray and cocktail cup set (#632). The tray measures 7.5" across the tab; the cocktail cup measures 2.25" high. *Courtesy of June Sakata Scoggins.* $135+ set

Hostess Ware Martini server (#630), with a molded number "630" on the base, 10.25" h. An advertisement in the 1935 *House & Garden* magazine described a set including the martini server as including, "A stirring cup to please the most exacting. Full quart in size and complete with a chromium spoon. Individual canape tray with convenient handle and fitted for cocktail cups. In six Pacific colors." *Courtesy of Robert R. Perry.* $350+

Canapé tray (#652) and cocktail cup (# 651) in cobalt glaze. The canapé tray is marked with an incised "Pacific 632," 8" w. to tab. The cocktail cup is unmarked, 2.25" h. *Courtesy of Walter Schirra Ceramics (calpottery@mindspring.com).* $135+ set

Rare ring pitcher (#430), unmarked, 8.5" h. *Courtesy of Robert R. Perry.* $300+

Ball jugs (#420), with circular marks. The mottled green glazed ball jug, incised with the number "420," is an early example. 9" h. each. *Courtesy of Robert R. Perry.* $125+ each

Orange ring pitcher (#430), 8.25" h.; four barrel tumblers (#431) in cobalt, yellow, orange, and light blue; yellow handled target tray (#413) to serve up the pitcher and tumblers, 15" d. *Courtesy of Mark Wiskow & Susan Strommer.* Pitcher: $300+; tumblers: $125+ each; target tray: $195

Ball jugs, 3 qt., most marked "Pacific Made In USA, 420," 9" h. However, the light blue ball jug is early and is marked only with an incised "Pacific 420." *Courtesy of Naomi's of San Francisco.* $125+ each

Tray (#612), 2 qt. water pitcher (#508), circular "Pacific Made In USA" mark 8" high to spout, and tumbers (#409). *Courtesy of Robert R. Perry.* Tray: $135; pitcher: $175; tumblers: $55+ each

Two quart pitcher (#508), unmarked, 8" h.; small 7 oz. tumblers, marked "Pacific 411" (impressed), with attachable handles (#1204), 4.5" h.; and a large "target" serving tray (#451), 15.75" d. *Courtesy of Robert R. Perry.* Pitcher: $175; tumblers: $25+ each; tray: $195

Graduated pitchers: two quart pitcher with lid (#508); one quart pitcher (#429), 5.25" h.; one pint pitcher (#428), 4.25" h.; and barrel shaped half pint pitcher with lid (#427), 3.5" h. *Courtesy of Mark Wiskow & Susan Strommer.* Left to right: $225, $95, $75, $95

Hostess Ware pitchers: two #508 2 qt. 8" h., one #428 1 pt. 5.25" h., and one #427 1/2 pt. 4.5" h. pitcher. *Courtesy of Robert R. Perry.* #508: $175; #428: $75; #427: $55

Same graduated pitchers in different colors: two quart green (#508), one quart light blue (#429), one pint orange (#428), and half pint yellow (#427). *Courtesy of Mark Wiskow & Susan Strommer.* Left to right: $175, $95, $75, $55

Tumbler, 7 oz., in an unusual Desert Brown glaze color displaying an impressed "Pacific 411" mark, 4.25" h. *Courtesy of Robert R. Perry.* $35

Hostess Ware graduated pitchers, 8" to 3.5" h. Both circular and impressed Pacific marks. *Courtesy of June Sakata Scoggins.* These pitchers range in value from $45 to $175.

Tray and three pitchers: The tray is marked "Pacific 617," 15" l. The pitchers measure 5", 4.5", and 3.25" high. The center pitcher is marked but illegible while the other two are unmarked. Pitchers: 1 qt. (#429), 5" h.; 1 pt. (#428), 4.5" h.; 1/2 pt. (#427), 3.25" h. With a lid, the smallest pitcher becomes a syrup pitcher (#308). There is a larger 2 qt. (#508) pitcher as well. *Courtesy of Naomi's of San Francisco.* Tray: $175; #429 pitcher: $95; #428 pitcher: $75; #427 pitcher: $55

Additional examples of Hostess Ware 7 oz. tumblers in various colors. Back, left to right: Royal (a.k.a. Pacific) Blue, Delphinium Blue, Aqua, Lemon (a.k.a. Canary) Yellow, Apache Red. Front, left to right: Apricot, Sierra White. *Courtesy of Naomi's of San Francisco.* $25+ each.

Back: white tab handled individual baker marked "Pacific Made In USA 205;" 1 pt. (#458) pitcher, 4" h.; pitcher (#460), 9" h. Front: sugar bowl, 4.25" h.; individual vegetable dish marked "Pacific Made In USA 667" (#666 is an individual salad dressing boat); individual melted butter dish with a molded mark "434" only. *Courtesy of Walter Schirra Ceramics (calpottery@mindspring.com).* Back, left to right: $25+, $45+, $95+. Front: NPD (**N**o **P**rice **D**etermined), $45+, $35+

Pitchers (#460 2 qt. and #458 1 pt.) in green and red respectively, circular "Pacific Made In USA" mark, 8.75" h. & 5.25" h. *Courtesy of Robert R. Perry.* #460: $95; #458: $45

Orange one pint pitcher (#459), 3.75" h.; turquoise three ring footed two quart pitcher (#460), 8.25" h. Not shown is the one quart pitcher. *Courtesy of Mark Wiskow & Susan Strommer.* Left to right: $45, $95

Two quart pitcher (#460), 9" h.; lidded sugar bowl (#463), 4" h. creamers (#464), and 3" h. individual creamers (#462). These pieces are identified with "Pacific" circular marks. *Courtesy of June Sakata Scoggins.* Pitcher: $95+; lidded sugar: $125; #464 creamers: $125; #462 creamer: $30

Top left: Nine ounce ball tumblers (#419); right: goblets (#431); bottom left: barrel tumblers (#431), ranging from 5.5" to 4.5" h. Black and sand glaze ball tumblers are very rare. *Courtesy of June Sakata Scoggins.* Tumblers: $55+ each; goblets: $125 each; barrel tumblers: $125+ each

Cobalt "antique type" 8 oz. tumbler (#418) and antique type 2.5 quart pitcher (#417). Mug: 3.5" h.; pitcher: 11.75" h. to lip. *Courtesy of Walter Schirra Ceramics (calpottery@mindspring.com).* Left to right: $25, $65

Unusual "antique type" tumbler (#418), marked "Pacific 418" (Pacific name impressed and catalog number 418 molded), 3.75" h. *Courtesy of June Sakata Scoggins.* $25

Three covered water bottles (#410), unmarked, 10" h. with the lid. *Left: courtesy of Walter Schirra Ceramics (calpottery@mindspring.com). Center: courtesy of Jimm Edgar & Bettie Dakotah. Right: courtesy of Naomi's of San Francisco.* $350+ with lid; $200 without lid

Yellow water bottle with lid, marked with an incised number "410," 10" h. with lid. *Courtesy of June Sakata Scoggins.* $350+

Buffet bottle, coffee bottle, tumblers and a goblet in cobalt. Top left: 2 qt. buffet bottle with cover (#453), unmarked, 8.5" h. Top right: coffee bottle with cover (#438), unmarked, 9" h. Bottom row, left to right: short 7 oz. tumbler, marked "Pacific Made In USA 411," 4.5" h.; tall tumbler, unmarked, 5" h.; barrel tumbler (#431), unmarked, 4" h.; footed goblet (#433), unmarked, 5.75" h. *Courtesy of Walter Schirra Ceramics (calpottery@mindspring.com).* Buffet bottle: $155; coffee bottle: $95+; 7 oz. tumbler: $25; tall tumbler: $35; barrel tumbler: $125; footed goblet: $125

Coffee bottle (#438) in Delphinium (light) blue, 9" h. *Courtesy of Mark Wiskow & Susan Strommer.* $95+

Lidded water bottle (#410) in Apricot, unmarked, 10.25" h. to lid. *Courtesy of Robert R. Perry.* $350+

Eight cup coffee bottles (#438) with cover and wooden and metal handles, 9" h. *Courtesy of June Sakata Scoggins.* $95+

Two Hostess Ware after dinner coffee pots (#442), the number 442 with both an impressed and circle mark, one on each pot, 9" h. each. *Courtesy of June Sakata Scoggins.* $225 each

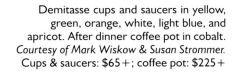

Demitasse cups and saucers in yellow, green, orange, white, light blue, and apricot. After dinner coffee pot in cobalt. *Courtesy of Mark Wiskow & Susan Strommer.* Cups & saucers: $65+; coffee pot: $225+

Two tall after dinner six cup coffee pots (#442) in orange and cobalt, 9" h., and a small, extremely rare, individual white demi coffee pot, 5.75" h. x 6.5" l. The lids are all interchangable. *Courtesy of Mark Wiskow & Susan Strommer.* $225+ each

Hostess Ware teapots: large (#447), 7.5" h. to finial x 9.75" spout to handle and small (#446), 5.5" h. to finial x 8" spout to handle. The large teapots are glazed in yellow and burnt orange (a rare glaze color). The small teapots are glazed in green, yellow and light blue. *Courtesy of Mark Wiskow & Susan Strommer.* $195+ each

A rare, early Hostess Ware coffee pot identified with a diamond shaped "Pacific Pottery" paper label, unmarked, 9.75" h. *Courtesy of Robert R. Perry.* $450+

Open sugar and two teapots: open sugar (#463), 3.75" h.; four cup teapot (#446), 6" h.; six cup teapot (#447), 7" h. *Courtesy of Robert R. Perry.* Left to right: $45, $195, $195

Large eight cup teapots (#440), 11.5" spout to handle x 5.75" h. Low individual teapots (#439), 7 7/8" spout to handle x 3.5" h. to finial. All of these teapots are glazed in orange and green. *Courtesy of Mark Wiskow & Susan Strommer.* $195+ each

Hostess Ware cobalt glazed eight cup teapot (#440), creamer, sugar, tea cup and saucer, and a rare coffee cup. Teapot, marked "Pacific Made In USA 440," 5.75" h.; creamer, marked "Pacific Made In USA 404;" sugar, unmarked; tea cup (#608) and saucer (#609), saucer marked "Pacific Made In USA 609," cup 2.75" h., saucer 5.75" d.; coffee cup (#634), unmarked, 3" h. *Courtesy of Walter Schirra Ceramics (calpottery@mindspring.com).* Teapot: $195+; sugar and creamer: $75 set; tea cup and saucer: $22+; coffee cup: $45

Condiment pot / jam pot (#448) with a chromium handle, unmarked, 4.25" h. without handle, 5.25" h. with handle; Hostess Ware low four cup teapot (#439) marked "Pacific 439," 4" h. Both items are glazed in Apricot, a rare color. *Courtesy of Ken Solus & Larry Holben.* $195+ each

Hostess Ware eight cup teapot (#440) glazed in Apricot, 11.5" l. x 5.5" h. *Courtesy of Robert R. Perry.* $195+

Cobalt teapot, sugar with a rare lid and creamer, a demitasse cup and saucer, and a tray. Teapot: unmarked, 3.5" h.; sugar, unmarked, 3.25" h.; creamer, unmarked, 2" h. to spout; demitasse cup, 2" h., saucer: 4.5" h., both unmarked; tray (#616), unmarked, 12.5" l. *Courtesy of Walter Schirra Ceramics (calpottery@mindspring.com).* Teapot: $195; sugar and creamer: $165+ set; demitasse cup and saucer: $65 set; tray: $125+

Cobalt sugar (#463) with lid and creamer (#464) set, both unmarked. Sugar: 4.75" h. *Courtesy of Walter Schirra Ceramics (calpottery@mindspring.com).* $125 set

Open sugars and creamers. Top: unusually large sized sugars (#403) and creamers (#404), 3" h. each. Bottom: Apricot sugar (#463) and creamer (#464); small individual sugars (#461) and creamers (#462). The sugars were sold either with lids or "open." *Courtesy of June Sakata Scoggins.* Top sets: $55 per set. Apricot set: $75. Individual sets: $75 per set

109

Full sized cobalt sugar (#403) and creamer (#404): sugar 3.25" h., creamer 4" h.; footed light green mini sugar and light blue mini creamer with tab handles: sugar 2 5/8" h., creamer 3" h.; orange flat mini sugar (#450) and creamer (#449) with tab handles, 2" h. each. *Courtesy of Mark Wiskow & Susan Strommer.* Full sized sugar and creamer set: $75+; mini sugar and creamer: $60 set; flat mini sugar and creamer: $60 set

Demitasse cup and saucer. Cup: 2.75" h.; saucer: 4.5" d. $65 set

Opposite page: Pacific did not forget the children when they designed Hostess Wares. Children's pieces with divided dish with molded bunny rim decoration (#656); bunny handled mush bowl (#657); and two handled mugs (#658). Divided dish: 9" d., bowl across handle: 6.5", mugs: 3" h. *Courtesy of June Sakata Scoggins.* $145+ each

A closer look at the range of Hostess Ware cups and saucers available and seen elsewhere among the photographs. Back row, left to right: turquoise coffee mug and saucer (possibly later period with unusual stepped rings and a bell shaped body style); orange coffee mug on saucer (this is the common piece, the same shape as the demi cup but larger, with a foot). Front row: tea cup and saucer in light blue, common; unusual coffee mug and saucer in green with a rounded body and handle to the cup; and a typical demi cup and saucer in cobalt. *Courtesy of Mark Wiskow & Susan Strommer.*

Scarce cobalt and green divided bunny plates (#656) for children, 9" d. *Courtesy of Mark Wiskow & Susan Strommer.* $145+ each

Decorated Ware

In the mid-1930s, Pacific developed a line of "decorated" wares featuring hand decorated designs applied over the company's established solid glaze colors. Hostess Ware bodies were used in this line. The company described the decorative treatments as "free hand fused decorations." The process required three trips through the kiln to complete. However, when the process was finished, the decorated wares were guaranteed not to craze and were ovenproof. Advertising for decorated ware reminded consumers to ask for Pacific pottery, identified by the diamond shaped paper label. In 1937, among the most popular Pacific decorated designs were Fruit, Poppy, and Wheat.

Service plate, turquoise with Grapes, 16" d.; service plate, yellow with wheat, 16" d. *Courtesy of Mark Wiskow & Susan Strommer.* $275+

Among the wares decorated in this way were service pieces, flower bowls, and vases. Decorative motifs available for this line included Chrysanthemum, Dimity, Fruit (offered in sets with a variety of fruit), Game (also offered in a set), Grape, Poinsettia, Poppy, Wheat, Wheat Spray, Willow, and Windmill. Geometric designs received less descriptive designations, including BG (known to collectors as "Plaid" today), 2007, and 2008.

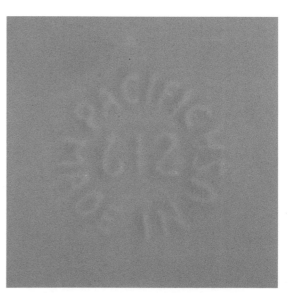

Poppy decorated large circular cake plate (#619) and a low bowl (#663), 13" d. and 12" d. *Courtesy of June Sakata Scoggins.* Left to right: $175, $125

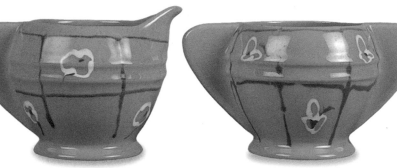

Dimity pattern, hand decorated small cream and sugar set decorated in the Trellis pattern. Creamer: 3" h. to rim. Open sugar (#449), marked "Pacific Made in USA." *Courtesy of Mark Wiskow & Susan Strommer.* $165+

Chrysanthemum decorated luncheon (9.75" d.) and dinner (11 3/8" d.) plates. *Courtesy of Mark Wiskow & Susan Strommer.* Luncheon: $95; dinner: $125

Fruit designs were offered in a seven piece Salad Set (catalog #111) and included apples, cherries, grapes, oranges, pears, and pineapples. The background glaze colors available for the pieces in this set were Green, White, and Yellow. This salad set included six 7.5" diameter salad plates (one each of each design to set) and one 12" low salad bowl.

Fruit designs were also offered on a seven piece Fruit Set (#113). Apples, cherries, and oranges decorated the wares of this set. The background colors available were, once again, Green, White, and Yellow. The set was comprised of six 5.5" diameter sauce dishes (two each of each design to a set) and one 8" diameter bowl.

The seven piece Game Set (#117) featured plates decorated with one duck each. Background colors available for this set included Delphinium, Red, Turquoise, White, and Yellow. The wares that made up the set included one 14" oblong platter and six 9" diameter plates.

A nine piece Salad Set (#104) was offered in the geometric designs 2007, 2008, and BG. Background colors for the nine piece set included Green, Red, White, and Yellow. The wares comprising the set included one 9" diameter salad bowl, six 7.5" diameter salad plates, and one wooden fork and spoon. In advertisements, pieces decorated in BG ("Plaid") were recommended for either Spring breakfasts or country and outdoor use.

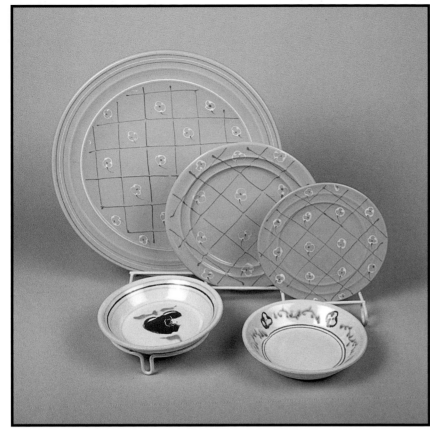

Dimity decorated plates, one fruit (apple) decorated sauce bowl, and an unidentified pattern sauce bowl. Plates: 11.5", 7.5" and 6" d. Two sauce bowls (#601), 5.5" d. *Courtesy of June Sakata Scoggins.* Plates: $125, $65, $45 respectively; sauce bowls: $45 each

Low salad server (#624), 15", with Poinsettia decoration. *Courtesy of Mark Wiskow & Susan Strommer.* $275

Turquoise service plate with Wheat decoration, 16" d. *Courtesy of Mark Wiskow & Susan Strommer.* $275+

"Blossoms:" 5.5" sauce dish (#601); 9.25" d. Poppy decorated plates (three, # 611), 11 3/8" d. dinner plate. *Courtesy of Mark Wiskow & Susan Strommer.* Sauce dish (#601): $45; plates (#611): $95+; dinner: $125

An eleven piece Coffee Set (#116) could be purchased decorated in either Wheat Spray on Blue, Green, White, or Yellow background glazes, or Willow on Turquoise, White, and Yellow. Pieces in the set included one buffet coffee bottle with a cover, four coffee tumblers with wooden handles, and one 15" diameter tray.

Buffet server (#453) decorated in Wheat Spray. 7" h. *Courtesy of Naomi's of San Francisco.* $145

Hand decorated red, white, and blue BG (or "Plaid") decorated circular platter, four footed bowl, two plates, and a rectangular tray. Platter, unmarked, 17.25" d.; footed bowl, marked "Pacific Made In USA 310," 9.25" d.; tray, marked incised "Pacific 616" and stamped "BG." Plates, 12.75" l.; large plate marked "Pacific 613" and stamped "BG," 11.25" d.; small plate marked "Pacific 611" and stamped "BG," 9.5" d. *(Platter and 4 foot bowl by Walter Schirra; rest by Naomi.) Courtesy of Walter Schirra Ceramics (calpottery@mindspring.com). Courtesy of Naomi's of San Francisco.* Platter: $295+; footed bowl: $95+; tray: $225+; 11.25" d. plate: $125+; 9.5" d. plate: $95+

Coffee bottle with cover (#438) decorated in the 2007 motif. 9.25" h. *Courtesy of Naomi's of San Francisco.* $155

Circle 2007 decorative motif: one ring cake plate, gray and white on orange, 12.75" d.; dinner plate, cobalt and white on light blue, 11" d.;. white on cobalt (broken rings), 7.5" d.; burnt orange and white on green, 6.25" d. *Courtesy of Mark Wiskow & Susan Strommer.* Left to right: $175, $125, $65, $45

Coffee set (#116—11 pieces complete) decorated in Wheat Spray: buffet server carafe and four small tumblers (#411). The tumblers measure 4.25" h. For this set, the bottom plate should have a center well for the carafe. *Courtesy of Mark Wiskow & Susan Strommer.* $695 set

A three piece Sunday Supper Set (#114) was decorated with either Windmill on White only; Chrysanthemum on Yellow only; or Wheat Spray on Green, Royal Blue, White, and Yellow. Pieces comprising the set included one 15" diameter tray and a one quart Bean Pot and Cover (decorated).

A nine piece Sunday Supper Service (#115) was also decorated with Windmill on White only; Chrysanthemum on Yellow only; or Wheat Spray on Green, Royal Blue, White, or Yellow. The wares making up this service included one 15" diameter tray, one 1 quart Bean Pot and Cover (decorated), and six 9" diameter plates.

Among the newer hand decorated wares for 1937 was a Pumpkin Pie Set including an oven-proof pie plate (for baking and serving) adorned with a central pumpkin motif and six individual pie plates. The oven-proof pie plate came with detachable wooden handles for easy handling. In 1937, the set sold for $5.95.

Pie plate (#638) with detachable wood handles, cobalt with pumpkin motif, 11" d. *Courtesy of Mark Wiskow & Susan Strommer.* $95+

Three hand decorated plates, 11.25" d. All three are marked with an impressed Pacific 611 mark. The right-hand plate also is hand marked XBM317. *Courtesy of Walter Schirra Ceramics (calpottery@mindspring.com).* $125 each

Chrysanthemum decorated luncheon (9.75" d.) and dinner (11 3/8" d.) plates. *Courtesy of Mark Wiskow & Susan Strommer.* Luncheon: $95; dinner: $125

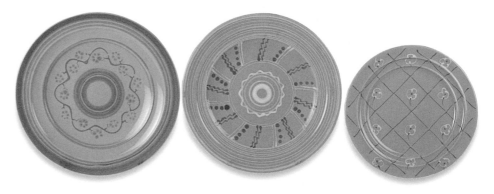

Three hand decorated plates: left: marked Pacific 611, 9.5" d.; center: hand marked XBN412 and impressed Pacific 611, 9.25" d.; right: marked Pacific 610 in raised lettering, 7.75" d. *Courtesy of Walter Schirra Ceramics (calpottery@mindspring.com).* Left to right: $95, $95, $65

Buffet server (#453) with Chrysanthemum decoration, cobalt and white on green. *Courtesy of Mark Wiskow & Susan Strommer.* $165+

Hand decorated wares: back row: plate with anchor marked with an impressed Pacific 613, 11" d.; rectangular tray with wheat motif and a molded "Pacific Made In USA 659" mark, 10.75" l. Front row: creamer and sugar, creamer marked "Pacific 404" and sugar marked "Pacific 403," 3" and 4" h. respectively; unmarked pitcher, green with blue and white trailed design, 3.5" h.; yellow ball tumbler, marked but illegible, 5" h. *Courtesy of Walter Schirra Ceramics (calpottery@mindspring.com)*. Back row: plate: $125+; tray: $195. Front row: creamer and sugar: $95 set; pitcher: $85; tumbler: $65

Salad plate, black with ship's wheel, 7.5" d.; cobalt salad plate with white sail boat, 7.5" d. *Courtesy of Mark Wiskow & Susan Strommer.* $65+ each

Footed coffee cups (#634) and a melted butter dish (#434), hand painted. The cobalt cup with the anchor motif is initialed "WBG" on the back. *Courtesy of June Sakata Scoggins.* Cups: $125+ each; dish: $45

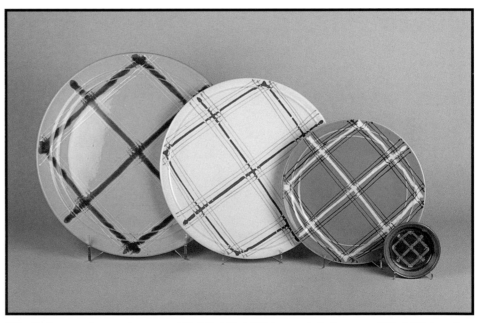

"Plaid" platters, plate, and coaster. 16", 14", 11", 4.25" (coaster) d. *Courtesy of Mark Wiskow & Susan Strommer.* 16": $275; 14": $225; 11": $125; 4.25": $45

Pacific "figural" plates. Dutch girl, salad plate (#610), 7.75" d.; 12.25" low salad server (#663), Dutch boy and girl (unusual to have boy), and 15.5" low salad server (#624) with Dutch girl. *Courtesy of Mark Wiskow & Susan Strommer.* Salad plate (#610): $65; low salad server (#663): $125; #624 low salad server: $275

Unusual burgundy on white "Plaid" place setting: 5.75" fruit bowl, bread and butter plate, salad plate, luncheon plate, tea cup and saucer, and 4.25" h. tumbler (#608-9). *Courtesy of Mark Wiskow & Susan Strommer.* Fruit bowl: $45; bread and butter plate: $45; salad plate: $65; luncheon plate: $95; tea cup and saucer: $125+ set.

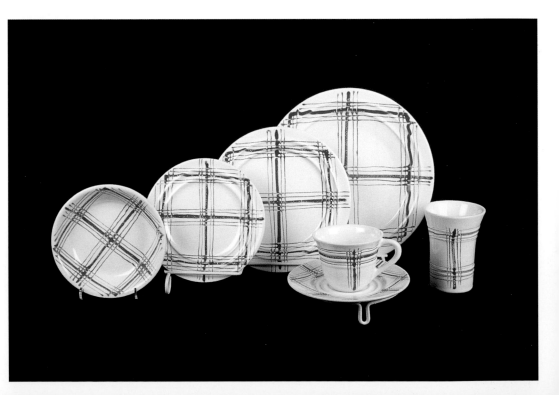

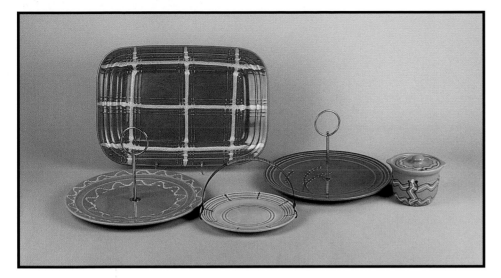

Serving pieces: rectangular platter (#617), white and green on orange, 15" (the largest of three platters in this rectangular form); center handle server, double "Sine Wave" white on light blue, 11" d.; center handle server, brown and white pussy willows and brown and white trim motifs, 11" d.; 7.5" d. server, cobalt and white "railroad tracks on yellow, " with a raffia wrapped spring handle (it is unusual to have the handle so small as to fit a 7" plate — usually they fit 12" diameter plates); condiment jar (with or without slot in lid), cobalt and white on light blue, "nervous or wiggly plaid" (unusual decoration), 3.5" h. x 5" across the tab handles. *Courtesy of Mark Wiskow & Susan Strommer.* Rectangular platter: $275; center handle servers: $125+ each; server with spring handle: $65; condiment jar: $195+

Two hand decorated plates (#611) with impressed "Pacific 611" manufacturer's marks, 9.5" d. The plate on the left is decorated in BG ("Plaid"). *Courtesy of June Sakata Scoggins.* $95 each

Decorated tea cups, 3" h. *Courtesy of Naomi's of San Francisco.* $65 each

BG ("Plaid") decorated 7.5" d. plate and a hand decorated ball tumbler, 5" h. *Courtesy of Naomi's of San Francisco.* Plate: $45; tumbler: $65

121

Flower pot decorated in a rust and yellow BG ("Plaid") motif on a green glaze coat, 4" d. *Courtesy of Mark Wiskow & Susan Strommer.* $75+

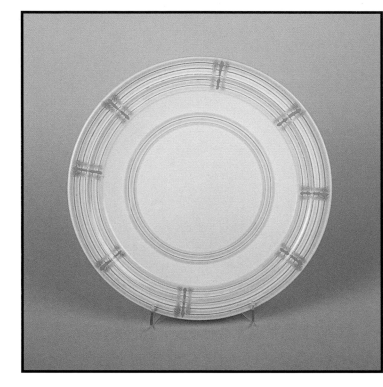

Pacific plate (#613) with a BF ("railroad tracks" or "spoke and wheel") decorative motif, marked with a "613 Pacific" incised mark and a rubber stamped "BF," 11" d. *Courtesy of Naomi's of San Francisco.* $125

BF ("railroad tracks" or "spoke and wheel") hand decorated wares: tray, marked "Pacific 617," 15" l.; creamer and sugar set marked "Pacific 450" on the creamer and "Pacific 449" on the sugar; 7 oz. tumbler, marked "Pacific Made IN USA 411," 4.25" h. *Courtesy of Walter Schirra Ceramics (calpottery@mindspring.com).* Tray: $275; cream and sugar: $165+ set; tumbler: $65

Punch/salad bowl (#310), gold and white BF decoration on green, 9.25" d, resting on an 11.25" d. dinner plate with "railroad tracks" decoration. *Courtesy of Mark Wiskow & Susan Strommer.* Bowl: $95+; plate: $125

Flower pot decorated with gold and white "railroad tracks," 6" d, resting on a green 11.25" d. dinner plate. *Courtesy of Mark Wiskow & Susan Strommer.* Flower pot: $95+; plate: $125

"Vines and buds" decoration: two ring cake plate, white on cobalt, 15 7/8" d.; one ring cake plate, white on cobalt, 13.75" d.;. white on green (more stylized) plate, 11" d.; cobalt on green plate, 7.5" d. *Courtesy of Mark Wiskow & Susan Strommer.* Left to right: $275+, $225, $125, $65

Motif with stars and center circles (or not): dinner, white and gold on orange, 11.25" d.; luncheon white on cobalt (no swirl), 9.25" d.; salad, white on orange with center swirl, 7.25" d.; bread and butter plate with center swirl, 6.25" d.; bread and butter plate white on yellow, 6.25" d. *Courtesy of Mark Wiskow & Susan Strommer.* Left to right: $125, $95, $65, $45, $45

Motif with stars and center circles (or not): dinner plate, orange with gray, 11" d.; luncheon plate, turquoise with cobalt and white with center swirl, 9" d.; salad plate, green with olive green, 7.5" d.; bread and butter plate, yellow with burgundy, 6.25" d.; bread and butter plate, turquoise with cobalt and white; 6.25" d. *Courtesy of Mark Wiskow & Susan Strommer.* Left to right: $125 to $45

Motif with stars and center circles (or not): dinner plate, orange with gold, 11" d.; luncheon plate, white on green with unusual border, 9" d.; salad plate, yellow with orange and mauve, 7.5" d.; bread and butter plate, cobalt with white decoration, 6.25" d.; bread and butter plate with swirl, turquoise with blue, 6.25" d. *Courtesy of Mark Wiskow & Susan Strommer.* Left to right: $125, $95, $65, $45, $45

2008 ("Sine Wave") pattern: one ring cake, burgundy on turquoise, no center lanterns, 12.5" d.; cobalt on turquoise plate, 11.25" d.; yellow on orange plate, 11.25" d.; luncheon plate, orange on yellow, 9.25" d. An ink stamped back mark provides the pattern numbers, "2007-8" (2007 is the ring pattern, 2008 is the "Sine Wave" pattern—in the second plate from the left the two motifs are combined, leading to this designation). *Courtesy of Mark Wiskow & Susan Strommer.* Left to right: $125, $125, $125, $95

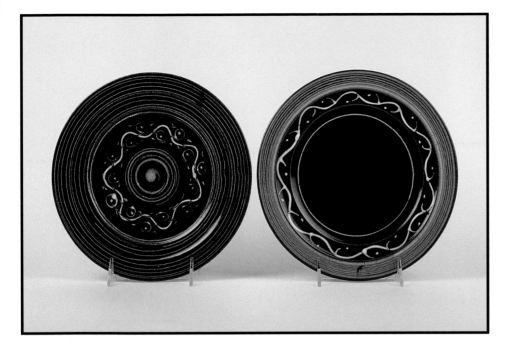

Top left: Hand decorated 9.25" d. plates. *Courtesy of Naomi's of San Francisco.* $95 each

Top right: One ring cake plate, cobalt on white, 14" d.; plate, white on cobalt 2008 ("Sine Wave" or "Hills and Valley" decoration by border, others call the center motif "Japanese Lantern"), 11.25" d.; luncheon plate, cobalt on apricot, 9.25" d.; melted butter dish (#434), rust on green (unusual rust), 4" d. *Courtesy of Mark Wiskow & Susan Strommer.* Left to right: $225, $125, $95, $45

Hand decorated plate, miniature creamer and sugar, and cup and saucer. Plate: 9.25" d.; creamer: 2.75" h.; cup: 3" h. *Courtesy of Naomi's of San Francisco.* $125 set

Hand decorated motifs adorn these low salad servers in orange with gray and yellow with orange, 17" d. each. *Courtesy of Mark Wiskow & Susan Strommer.* $295+

Low footed salad bowl (#314) decorated in cobalt and white. 12" d. *Courtesy of Mark Wiskow & Susan Strommer.* $95+

Hand decorated plates: left marked Pacific 610, 7.5" d.; center: unmarked, 7.5" d.; right: marked Pacific 612 and stamped 2007-4, 6.5" d. *Courtesy of Walter Schirra Ceramics (calpottery@mindspring.com).* Left to right: $65, $65, $45

Very atypical pieces. Salad plate, white on orange center spiral divided in quarters with dots, 7.5" d. Salad plate, green on white with an unusual medallion decoration and a possible HMC signature, 7.5" d. *Courtesy of Mark Wiskow & Susan Strommer.* $75+

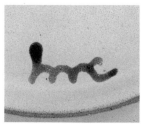

Orange hand decorated service plate,
17.25" d. *Courtesy of Mark Wiskow & Susan Strommer.* $295+

Luncheon plate, hand decorated, "Tennis Net", 9.25" d.; turquoise, blue, and white "Sine Wave" luncheon plate; dinner plates, 11" d., in yellow, orange, and white; "Harlequin" 13 5/8" service piece. *Courtesy of Mark Wiskow & Susan Strommer.* Luncheon plate: $95; dinner plate: $125; service piece: $225

Punch/salad bowl, burnt orange on green, 11" d. Both the bowl and plate are decorated in a variation of the "Vines and Blossoms" motif. The no ring plate the punch/salad bowl rests upon measures 17.25" d. *Courtesy of Mark Wiskow & Susan Strommer.* Bowl: $125+; plate: $295

Punch/salad bowl (#311), 11" d. (comes in 9", 11", and 14" ds), gold on orange, resting upon a 17.5" d. no ring plate. Both pieces are signed hmc. *Courtesy of Mark Wiskow & Susan Strommer.* Bowl: $125+; no ring plate: $295

Salad plates (2) with "spider web" decoration, 7.5" d.; dinner plates, 11" d. *Courtesy of Mark Wiskow & Susan Strommer.* Salad plates: $65; dinner plates: $125

Coralitos

Left: *Better Homes and Gardens* Pacific advertisement dating from October 1937 and featuring decorated wares. *Courtesy of Bill Harmon, Nine Lives Antiques.*

Bottom left: Coralitos set advertisement. It reads "An Enduring Gift From California. Coralitos 32 Piece Pottery Set. $14.95. Straight from California comes the most ideal of all Christmas gifts . . . a pottery service for six in warm, glowing colors, beautifully packaged in the wine colored, lacquered box decorated simply with the white flames of the flowering yucca . . . the "Candles of the Lord" that dot the hillsides of California. * A gift you may be proud to give . . . happy to receive. Coralitos pottery is wafer-thin yet durable, each piece carries a factory guarantee of quality. The gift set includes six 9 inch plates, six 6 inch plates, six cream soups, six cups and saucers, one 14 inch chop plate and one round vegetable bowl. It is available in all of the six Coralitos colors . . . Mission ivory, Cielito blue, coral, DuBonnet, Dorado yellow, and Verdugo green . . . or in a number of attractive combinations of these colors. You will find the stores featuring Coralitos gift sets listed on the opposite page. Pacific Pottery from California. Made by Pottery Division, Pacific Clay Products *** Los Angeles, California." *Courtesy of Bill Harmon, Nine Lives Antiques.*

Bottom center: The other side of the advertising folder lists the Coralitos dinnerware line in detail. It reads: "Top row: reading left to right: X14 14-in chop plate $1.75, X10 10-in dinner plate .75, X33 Individual creamer .60, X32 Individual sugar .65, X38 15-in platter $1.75, X31 Individual teapot $1.50, X23 5 1/2-in flat fruit dish .30, X24 7 1/2-in Nappie $1.00, X6 6-in bread-and-butter plate .35, X7 7-in dessert plate .45, X8 8-in salad plate .60, X9 9 1/2-in luncheon plate .65; Middle row: left to right: X40 After-dinner cup. ea. .35, X 41 After-dinner saucer.ea. .20, X39 After-dinner coffee pot $1.85, X42 7 1/2-in vegetable dish $1.25, X42-C Cover for vegetable dish $1.00, X27 Salt shaker .50, X28 Pepper shaker .50, X21 Handled soup bowl .50, X21-A Plain soup bowl .35, X26 Oval vegetable dish $1.75, X26-C Cover for vegetable dish .75, X4 Tea cup .40, X5 Saucer for tea cup .25, X1 Tea pot (6-cup) $1.85, X3 Large creamer .70, X2 Large sugar .80, X2-C Cover for sugar .25; Bottom row: left to right: X25 10-in salad bowl $1.85, X37 5-piece relish set with tray $3.95, X22 Gravy boat and tray $1.85, X30 Coffee mug .50, X29 Coffee bottle (8-cup) $1.85, X34 Toast cover $1.00, X8 8-in. plate .60." *Courtesy of Bill Harmon, Nine Lives Antiques.*

Arrangement of Coralitos ware in a rare glaze color: platter (X38), 15" l.; carafe; tumblers with wood and metal handles; plate; cup and saucer; and open sugar and creamer. *Courtesy of June Sakata Scoggins.* These pieces range in value from $6+ to $85+.

Coralitos luncheon, salad, bread and butter plates, nappy (X24) and flat fruit (X23) bowls. 9.5" d. luncheon plate; 7.5" d. nappy bowl (X24), 5.5" d. fruit bowl (X23). *Courtesy of June Sakata Scoggins.* Luncheon: $35; salad: $12; bread and butter: $8; nappy: $16

Pacific had a right to be satisfied with the enthusiastic public response to their Hostess Ware line. However, by 1937 consumers were looking for thinner bodied wares and new designs. Glaze colors sought after were described by industry reporter H. V. Kaeppel in his column "The Roving Reporter on the West Coast" as " . . . solid colors about halfway between pastel and bright. The ware has a high gloss." Kaeppel also provided his analysis of this change in public taste, "This transition is a reflection of the greater discrimination on the part of the buyer." (Kaeppel 1938, 62)

Responding to the public's desire for new wares with different designs and glazes, Pacific introduced the Coralitos line in 1937. The body of the new Coralitos line was described as "wafer-thin" and it was offered in four glaze colors. In time, six glaze colors were offered for the line, including Cielito Blue, Coral, DuBonnet, Verdugo Green, Mission Ivory, and Dorado Yellow. As an introductory offer, Pacific initially sold Coralitos salt and peppers for twenty-five cents. Once customers were hooked, these shakers were priced at one dollar a set.

A thirty-two piece set of Coralitos was available for $14.95 and included six 9" diameter plates, six 6" diameter plates, six cream soups, six cups and saucers, one 14" diameter chop plate, and one round vegetable bowl. When discussing prices for sets, Pacific was quick to remind cost-conscious Depression era customers that their wares were "surprisingly moderate in price," ranging from fifteen cents for an individual coaster to three dollars for a 15" decorated chop plate.

Coralitos handled soup bowl (X21), salad bowl (X25), vegetable dish (X42), and salt and pepper shaker. Bowls: 10" to 7.5" d. *Courtesy of June Sakata Scoggins.* Soup bowl: $25; salad bowl: $65; vegetable dish: $45; shakers: $20 each

Coralitos after dinner coffee pot, teapot, cup and saucer, tumbler with handle, coffee mug, cream and covered sugar set, and individual cream and open sugar set. *Courtesy of June Sakata Scoggins.* Coffee pot: $85; teapot: $65; cup and saucer: $15 set; tumbler: $15; mug: $15; cream and sugar: $45 set; individual cream and open sugar: $35 set

Coralitos packing box provides a useful backdrop for this Coralitos demitasse after dinner coffee pot and demitasse cups and saucers. The box once contained a 32 piece set. Coralitos was produced in six glaze colors: Mission ivory, Cielito blue, coral, DuBonnet, Dorado yellow, and Verdugo green. *Courtesy of June Sakata Scoggins.* Coffee pot: $85; cups and saucers: $20 each set

Coralitas toast cover set marked "Pacific Made In USA X34," 5.5" h. and after dinner coffee pot. *Toast cover set courtesy of Ken Solus & Larry Holben. After dinner coffee pot courtesy of Walter Schirra Ceramics (calpottery@mindspring.com).* Toast cover set: $65; coffee pot: $85

Toby-style pitchers, unmarked, 4" h. A paper label on side of upper pitcher is marked "Pacific Pottery California Product" and in the center "Coralitos Ware." *Courtesy of June Sakata Scoggins.* $85+ each

Corilitos salt (X27) and pepper (X28) shakers on a low artware bowl (#854), 12" d. x 2" h. The shakers are either unmarked or feature a molded "Pacific Made In USA" manufacturer's mark. *Courtesy of June Sakata Scoggins.* Shakers: $20 each; bowl: $55

Arcadia

Arcadia was another tableware line offered by Pacific at roughly the same time as Coralitos. This line was also designed to meet the public desire for thinner wares, different designs, and new glaze colors.

Arcadia dinner, luncheon, and bread and butter plates in the six colors offered. *Courtesy of June Sakata Scoggins.* These plates range in value from $8 to $45 by diameter.

Arcadia line: covered butter; 12" l. platter, marked with a diamond shaped stamped Arcadia Ware mark; 7.5" l. x 4" h. covered light blue sugar and 3" h. creamer set, marked with a circular "Pacific Made In Calif. USA" stamped mark; 4" h. dark blue sugar bowl (E2). *Courtesy of June Sakata Scoggins.* Covered butter: $45; platter: $45; sugar and creamer set: $45 set; sugar bowl: $20+

Unusual Arcadia salad plate (E8), and cups and saucers in all the line's colors. Plate: 8" d. *Courtesy of June Sakata Scoggins.* Plate: $12; cup and saucer: $15+ set

Arcadia salt and pepper shakers in a low artware bowl (#854). Shakers: 2.75" h. *Courtesy of June Sakata Scoggins.* Shakers: $15 each; bowl: $55

Arcadia covered coffee bottles (E29), 8.75" h.; two pitchers (E48), 6" h. and (E47), 4.5" h.; and a creamer (E3), 3" h. These pieces features a circular "Arcadia Made In USA" mark. *Courtesy of June Sakata Scoggins.* Coffee bottles: $65; E48 pitcher: $55; E47 pitcher: $45; creamer: $12

Arcadia coffee bottle and cups (E45) with metal and wood handles. *Courtesy of June Sakata Scoggins.* Coffee bottle: $65; cups: $15 each

Dura-Rim

In c. 1940, Pacific added the Dura-Rim dinnerware line to their offerings. Apparently, "wafer thin bodies" had rims that were easily chipped. As the Dura-Rim name suggests, the rims were rolled to make them more durable and chip-resistant. The sturdy Dura-Rim line was offered in six glaze colors.

Dura-Rim platter, plates, bowls, cup and saucer, and salt and pepper shakers. *Courtesy of June Sakata Scoggins.* Platter: $45; large bowl: $16; small bowl: $12; cup and saucer: $15 set; shakers: $15 each

Dura-Rim wares in Arcadia shape. Platter, carafe, teapot, cream and sugar. Platter: 12.5" d. *Courtesy of June Sakata Scoggins.* Platter: $45; carafe: $65; teapot: $65; cream and sugar: $35 set

Top left: Dura-Rim two tone and solid glaze wares. Platter: 13" d. Large bowl: 8" d. *Courtesy of June Sakata Scoggins.* Platter: $45; large bowl: $35; 7" and 8" d. plates: $8-12; cup and saucer: $15 set; shakers: $15 each

Bottom left: Large Dura-Rim platter with molded bell-shaped flower decoration and marked in ink "Dura-Rim by Pacific Made in Calif. USA," 13" d. *Courtesy of Walter Schirra Ceramics (calpottery@mindspring.com).* $25

Hand Painted Wares

By 1940, the public had become enamored with hand painted dinnerwares. In c. 1941 (the year Pacific's designer Robert E. Haynes would display a 31" diameter, 3.5" deep bowl filled with five gallons of water and six dozen gladioli at a pottery show), Pacific offered tablewares adorned with hand painted decorations in the following motifs: California Grape, Hibiscus, Shasta Daisy, and Strawberry. The Hibiscus motif adorned vases as well as tablewares.

These patterns and other Pacific wares were available for viewing and purchase in "leading stores," in Pacific's showroom at their main office (located at the 306 W. Avenue, Los Angeles address of their primary pottery plant), or at showrooms in New York City (160 Fifth Avenue) and the Chicago Merchandise Mart.

Molded and hand painted Hibiscus pattern place setting with a molded basket weave rim, molded salt and pepper shakers, and an ashtray. 13.25" d. chop plate to 6" d. plate. *Courtesy of June Sakata Scoggins.* Plates range in value from $10 to $55 with the increasing diameter of the plate. Salt and pepper: $55; ashtray: $20

Molded and painted California Grape pattern plates, covered butter, salt and pepper, saucer, and ashtray. Plates: 10.75" d. to 6" d. Salt and pepper: 2.5" l. Three different marks were used, two included "Pat. Pending." The plates range in value from $10 to $24 as the plate diameter increases. *Courtesy of June Sakata Scoggins.* Covered butter: $95; salt and pepper: $55 set; saucer: $5; ashtray: $20

Note the extra Hibiscus flower on the large 13.5" d. tray. Molded and hand painted decoration. *Courtesy of June Sakata Scoggins.* $75

Plates, low bowl, cup and saucer, and covered butter dish in raised and painted Strawberry pattern, ink stamped "Pacific Made In Calif. USA." mark. Plates: 10.75" and 6" d. *Courtesy of June Sakata Scoggins.* Plates: $24, $10; low bowl: $18; cup and saucer: $22 set; covered butter: $95

Dinnerware set decorated with hand painted Mexican motifs. The 10" diameter plates are marked "Pacific Made In USA E10." The 7" diameter plates are marked "Pacific Made In USA E7." The cups are marked "Pacific Made In USA 1060," 4.5" d. x 2.75" h. One piece features an apparent "MB" artist's mark as well. *Courtesy of Rick Hudson, "Hudson's," Berkeley, California.* $12-40 per piece depending on size and type.

Hand painted decoration with a "comical bear and bird" adorns this plate, ink stamp marked "Pacific Made In Calif. USA" and mold marked "E 8 Made In USA," 8" d. *Courtesy of June Sakata Scoggins.* $24

Decal Decorated Wares

Late in the game, Pacific also provided wares decorated with a variety of decals. French Ivy was introduced as a pattern in 1941.

French Ivy pattern oval platter, with a red transfer printed ivy pattern, marked "Pacific Pat. Pend Made In Calif. USA," 16.5" l. *Courtesy of June Sakata Scoggins.* $85

Hand painted Lily of the Valley pattern adorns platters, plates, and one bowl. These pieces are marked with a rectangular "hand painted" stamped mark on back. Plates range from 13" d. to 7" d. The bowl is marked with a "Pat. Pending" stamp mark. The green edged plates have rounder and thicker rims whereas the red trimmed ware has a downturned, narrow rim. *Courtesy of June Sakata Scoggins.* Plates range in value from $18 to $55 with the increasing diameter of the plate. Bowl: $18

Lily of the Valley pattern platters, oval covered casserole, and oval vegetable dish. Platters: 16" to 12" l. Covered casserole: 8" d. Vegetable dish: 10.5" l. *Courtesy of June Sakata Scoggins.* Platters range in value from $55 to $85 with the increasing size of the platter. Casserole: $55; vegetable dish: $45

This decal floral pattern marries Arcadia and Coralitos body shapes. Coralitos teapot and two cups and saucers. Teapot: 7.5" h.; saucer: 6" d. and cup: 4.5" d. *Courtesy of June Sakata Scoggins.* Teapot: $125; cup and saucer: $22 set

Sarong

Late in 1941, as America was about to be drawn into World War II, it was reported that Pacific Clay Products was moving ahead with a modernization program that would significantly increase the company's output in 1942. The firm had many new ideas for both dinnerware and artware designs. Twenty-five dinnerware lines were projected for 1942, complete with a variety of new shapes designed by well known California sculptors. One of the decal adorned lines produced in 1942 was Sarong. Sarong was described as a "short line buffet service" decorated in an "over-all primitive design characteristic of the South Seas." (*Ceramic Industry* 1942, 36)

Plates, cup and saucer in a Tiger Lily pattern, ink stamped "Pacific Made In Calif. USA." Plates: 10.75", 9.75"; and 6" d. Saucer: 5.75" d. Cup: 3.75" d. *Courtesy of June Sakata Scoggins.* Plates: $24, $24, $10. Cup and saucer: $22 set

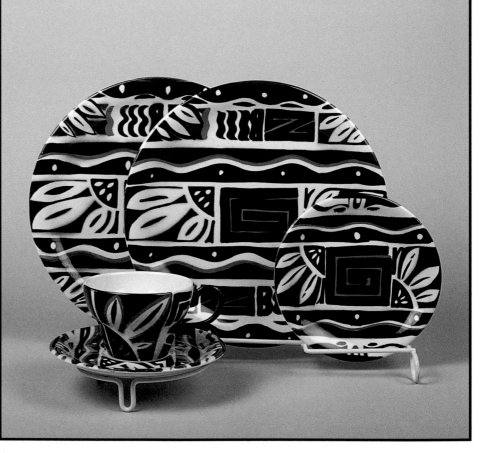

Sarong line, introduced in 1942, 10" and 6" d. plates, cup and saucer. 10" d. *Courtesy of June Sakata Scoggins.* Plates: $45 each; 6" d. plate: $12; cup and saucer: $45 set

The Final Offerings of 1942

In January 1942, potters at the Los Angeles Fifteenth Semi-Annual Gift & Art Show reported a significant increase in the volume of purchases among buyers. This was attributed to a combination of post-Christmas restocking, preparation for an anticipated paucity of ceramic wares available in months to come, and an increase in purchasing power related to the rising war time economy. Quality wares were said to be in greater demand than ever before.

The war years would present pottery firms with unusual opportunities and unprecedented challenges. In February 1942, it was reported that there was an upsurge in demand for American made semi-porcelain dinner services for twelve in the twenty-five dollar price range. These services had been provided by the Japanese before the war. Stimulated by the rising war time economy, potteries in February 1942 also saw an increased demand for higher priced tablewares.

Faced with the uncertainties of war, however, pottery manufacturers quickly simplified their lines and limited themselves to their most popular patterns. Few new dinnerware shapes were actually offered in 1942, as most firms stuck with their most successful lines of 1941. It was believed that this combination was most likely to allow potteries to fill orders quickly and provide better deliveries.

Viktor Schreckengost, designer for both American Limoges and Salem China, described what he believed would be the general stylistic trend for the war years: "It looks as if we are returning to the sentimental, dainty, and more colorful styles and decorations, as exemplified by the 18th Century school of design. This is a direct influence of the war. In such periods, people discover they have hearts after all, and they yearn for the things which harmonize with their emotions. For the duration of the war, the 18th Century influence will be predominant in practically all household furnishings." (Gibney 1942, p. 36)

Nationally, pottery firms faced challenges they had not seen before. Keeping an adequate labor force together to produce pottery was a great challenge. Men and women alike were leaving pottery firms for the battle fields and armament factories in droves. Some factories hired high school boys part time to help produce pottery and maintain the facilities. Of course, women not manufacturing munitions were working in factories in greater numbers than before, filling slots left by men recruited into the armed forces. In 1942, Gladding, McBean & Company would state that they had done all they could to accommodate the growing number of women working in the plant and could do no more!

In June of 1942, potters feared they would have next to nothing new to show the public. At the Atlantic City Pottery and Housewares Show in New Jersey, there was some question as to whether the show was worth holding at all. Many pottery firms were reluctant to commit themselves to displaying their limited wares and were unsure whether there would be adequate transportation to get them there and back. Considering how popular such shows were prior to the war, both as vehicles to capture the attention of consumers and keep track of the competition, the reluctance among potters to attend was quite significant.

Finally, there was great fear that in the coming war years cold weather would reduce or eliminate access to the natural gas supply necessary to fire the kilns. It was quickly seen that a cold snap could cripple production during winter months.

At the beginning of 1942, trade journals reported that Pacific offered some twenty-three different dinnerware patterns. These dinnerwares featured hand painted underglazed decorations. Thornberry was one of the pattern lines, described as having hand painted brown and green leaves with red berries over an ivory base. Vaguely described, two "Swedish-type" dinnerware lines were also offered. Arcadia would remain among the wares Pacific offered in that final year.

Despite the troubling prospect of difficult years to come, Pacific Clay Products put on a bold face and streamlined their operations, investing in some $15,000 worth of improvements to the main office. Vice president and general sales manager A.T. Wintergill felt that modernization of the facility at that time gave Pacific an air of progressiveness. A new shop would also be added to the company's operations at 2355 Norwalk Boulevard, Los Angeles. (*Ceramic Industry* 1942, 40)

Nevertheless, in August 1942, it was reported that Pacific had turned much of its capacity over to the production of war materials for the government. Even so, the company insisted that seven dinnerware patterns would continue to be produced. Those patterns included Belleaf, Brownbell, Grape, Hibiscus, Leopard Lily, Sarong, and Strawberry.

In October of 1942, however, pottery production at Pacific ceased and would not return. For the duration of the Second World War, Pacific Clay Products Company manufactured steatite porcelain (a component in high frequency radios) for the government. Pacific gave this product the trade name "SteaPACtite."

ARTWARE/FLORISTWARE:
POTTERY AROUND THE HOUSE AND IN PUBLIC SPACES, 1932-1942

X Olympiad 1932-Los Angeles California medallion marked with a "Pacific" and sunburst mark. Marked in a ring around edge of this medallion is "Pacific-Clay-Products." In the banner is the phrase "Citius Altius Fortiu." 7" d. Very rare. *Courtesy of the collection of Steve Temme & Dan Craver.* NPD

In 1932, Pacific Clay Products Company plunged into the artware market with enthusiasm. The company produced a wide range of artware products, including bowls, candlesticks, cigarette boxes, figurines, flower frogs, garden pots, planters, sand jars, and vases. These items ranged in size from the diminutive to the enormous. Prior to 1932, the company had produced a number of vases as well. Two of the designers responsible for Pacific's artwares during the 1930s were Bernita Lundy and the previously mentioned Robert E. Haynes. "Artware" or "art pottery," as it is used here, refers to factory-produced, decorative ceramics of striking designs that are either hand decorated or glazed in fashionable colors. Many of the company's early artware vases where hand thrown, while the later examples were slip molded.

Prior to pastel colors becoming the vogue in the latter half of the 1930s, Pacific's artwares were generally offered in Matte Green, Matte Ivory, Lustre Turquoise, and Lustre Yellow. In 1935, these colors were also listed as "Neptune Green, Ivory, Powder Blue, and Lemon Yellow." Additional colors were added over time, including a burgundy, a light blue described today as "shot with dots," a forest green, and a mustard yellow. (Wiskow 1999) In fact, for a price, a buyer could order artwares in any of the Hostess Ware glaze colors as well as

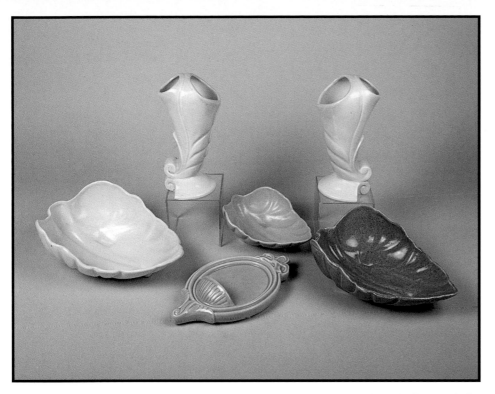

An example of Pacific artwares. Two vases, one wall pocket, and three leaf bowls: Bowls: 10.5";
10" and 7" l; vases: 8" h.; wall pocket: 9" l. *Courtesy of June Sakata Scoggins.* $45-65 each

In 1940, Pacific displayed some fifty new artware products at the Los Angeles Summer Gift and Art Show. The glaze colors featured were described as "dusty pink, rose, sea foam green, turquoise, and white." One design drew a lot of attention. It was a combination piece, a pair of bookends that doubled as either hanging or standing flower vases. Also displayed were artware bowls and vases in two-tone glazes. These pieces featured ivory glazed exteriors and colored interiors.

In early 1942, artwares produced by American potters were praised for the many new designs and for decorative wares patriotically assessed as superior in every way to the foreign imports no longer arriving on American shores. In early 1942, Pacific artware offerings included Royal Victory, a line of low bowls in twelve shapes with six blended glaze finishes. Robert Haynes was busy producing large, decorative low bowls. These accompanied a new line of figurines including animals and birds with a variety of glaze treatments. As a touch of whimsy during the upheavals of war, Pacific also released terra cotta Siamese Cats (life sized) and miniature hobby horses.

However, as previously discussed in the Tablewares & Kitchenwares chapter, in an increasingly difficult market with limited resources available to the company, insufficient manpower to support the artware lines, and increasing demands placed upon the company by the government to produce war related materials, Pacific announced in June 1942 that the artware lines would no longer be featured in company showrooms around the country. Those showrooms were closed and sales were handed over to an unnamed national jobber. Then, in October 1942, artware production ceased as Pacific Clay Products staff turned their efforts to the manufacture of steatite for high frequency radios to be used in the war.

Ashtrays & Cigarette Boxes

In 1935, Pacific advertised artware cigarette boxes and ashtrays with a unique circular body shape. Along with a range of artwares, these were described as coming in dainty finishes in pastels and ivory; specifically, the glazes were an exquisite pale blue, cool green, mellow ivory, and creamy yellow. These smoking accessories were further described as smartly informal and moderately priced.

the special order colors. This significantly increased the range of colorful glazes available to consumers looking for Pacific artwares.

Although not displayed in this book, Pacific added wall tiles to their list of new products available in June of 1937. Wall tile was found to be both aesthetically pleasing to consumers and labor saving to landlords. With wall tile in place, less maintenance was required annually as the walls covered in durable tiles did not need to be repainted when tenants left. Collectors should be on the lookout for Pacific wall tiles.

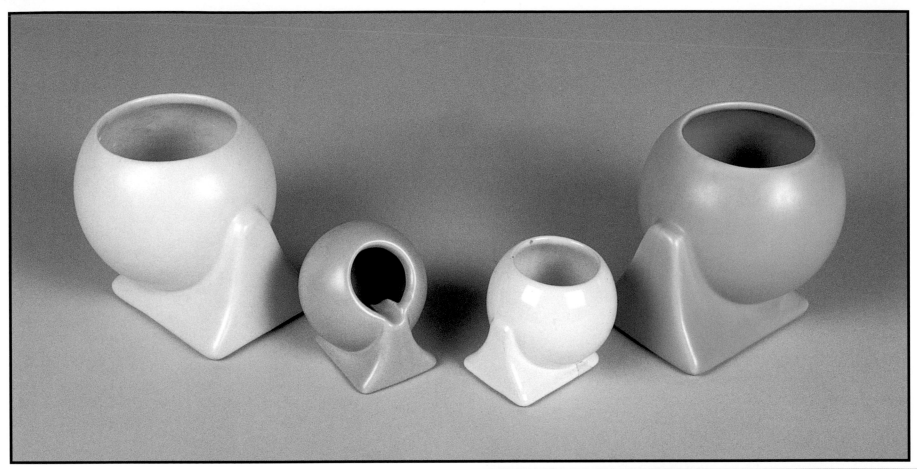

Small blue spherical ashtray (#45), 2.75" h., match holder (#67), 2.75" h., and cigarette holders (#68—back), 4" h. The ashtray is marked with an impressed "Pacific" manufacturer's mark and the number. The rest are marked with the circular Pacific mark. *Courtesy of June Sakata Scoggins.* Ashtray: $95, match holder: $95; cigarette holders: $125 each

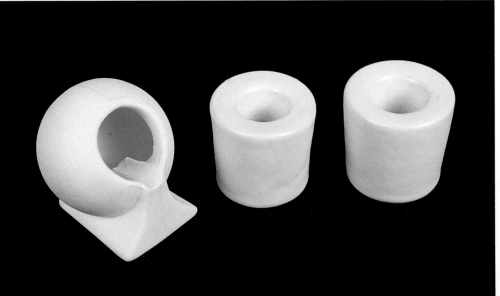

Spherical ashtray (#45) in bisque; white candle holders (#855). *Courtesy of Mark Wiskow & Susan Strommer.* Ashtray: $95; candle holders: $55 pair

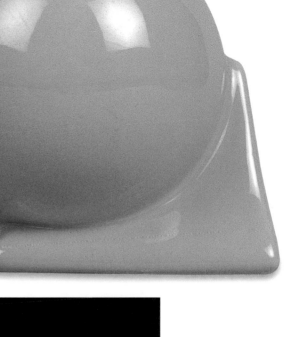

Bowls

A variety of artware bowls were produced by Pacific. A number of these can be found in use throughout this book. A fine example of an artware low bowl is seen holding large numbers of Hostess Ware and Coralitos salt and paper shakers.

"Saturn" bowls. "Saturn" bowl (#701) in matte white, 12.5" dia x 3.5" h.; "Saturn" bowl (#701), unusual medium blue "shot with dots;" very unusual Fulper-like* blue glaze "Saturn" bowl (#700), 9.5" d.; and "Saturn" bowl (#700), somewhat unusual early green glaze, 9.5" d. x 2.5" h. (*Fulper pottery company, Flemington, New Jersey, 1858-1935. For more on Fulper, see Snyder, *Depression Pottery,* 1999, pp. 75-76.) *Courtesy of Mark Wiskow & Susan Strommer.* #701 bowls: $125+; #700 bowls: $95+

"Saturn" bowls. "Saturn" bowl (#700) in matte yellow, matte white, and gloss orange; "Saturn" bowl (#701), Pacific blue and gloss yellow. Each bowl measures 9.5" d. *Courtesy of Mark Wiskow & Susan Strommer.* #700: $95+; #701: 125+

Candlesticks & Console Bowls

A short item about Pacific's flower and candle set. The caption reads: "A flower and candle set that does tricks. In the hands of a smart hostess, there's practically no end to the unusual combinations that can be achieved with these attractive pieces. And here's a thought: It may be purchased as an ensemble of ten pieces, as illustrated, or each piece may be bought as desired. Complete ensemble, $10.00." The accompanying article reads: "From the Days of the Spanish Dons. *Piquantly suggestive of the romantic Spanish era in the early history of California, yet blended subtly with modern trends in decoration, the rich warm tones of Pacific Potteries create a feeling of easy hospitality and gracious living. Gayly informal, their lively colors and simple design add a welcome note of spontaneity to any gathering.

Only native California clays are used in fashioning these pieces. Because of the fine earthen ware body, each article will withstand hard wear and can be used for cooking as well as serving. Pacific offers pottery to fulfill every hostess' need, including complete table and buffet service, an interesting variety of ornamental and garden pieces and practical kitchen ware. Each article finished in five different glazes — Lemon Yellow, Apache Red, Pacific Blue, Jade Green, Sierra White. These colors, used singly or in harmonious combination, give informality its most attractive setting.

Reproductions of a few Pacific pieces are shown in this folder in popular color combinations." *Courtesy of Bill Harmon, Nine Lives Antiques.*

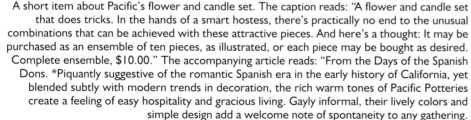

A flower and candle set that does tricks. In the hands of a smart hostess, there's practically no end to the unusual combinations that can be achieved with these attractive pieces. And here's a thought: It may be purchased as an ensemble of ten pieces, as illustrated, or each piece may be bought as desired. Complete ensemble, $10.00.

From the Days of the Spanish Dons

Piquantly suggestive of the romantic Spanish era in the early history of California, yet blending subtly with modern trends in decoration, the rich, warm tones of Pacific Potteries create a feeling of easy hospitality and gracious living. Gayly informal, their lively colors and simple design add a welcome note of spontaneity to any gathering.

Only native California clays are used in fashioning these pieces. Because of the fine earthen ware body, each article will withstand hard wear and can be used for cooking as well as serving. Pacific offers pottery to fulfill every hostess' need, including complete table and buffet service, an interesting variety of ornamental and garden pieces and practical kitchen ware. Each article finished in five different glazes—Lemon Yellow, Apache Red, Pacific Blue, Jade Green, Sierra White. These colors, used singly or in harmonious combination, give informality its most attractive setting.

Reproductions of a few Pacific pieces are shown in this folder in popular color combinations.

Ten piece flower and candle set (#712, #713, #714). The components may be rearranged in any number of creative ways to create a most impressive centerpiece. The complete set is very rare. *Courtesy of Peter S. Amantea.* $300++

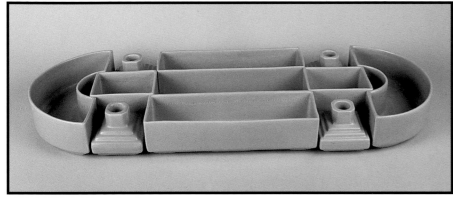

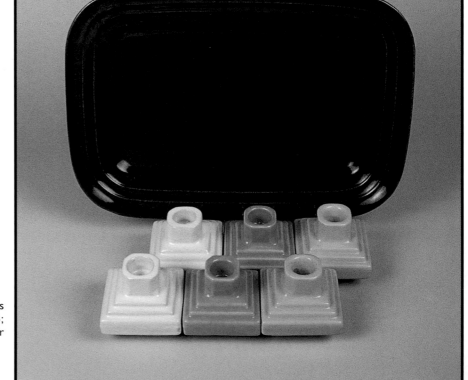

Tray (#617), 14.5" l., and six square candle holders (#715). *Courtesy of June Sakata Scoggins.* Tray: $175; candleholders: $90 pair

Cobalt candle holders (#715), unmarked, 3" h. *Courtesy of Walter Schirra Ceramics (calpottery@mindspring.com).* $90 pair

Candle holders, all unmarked. The footed candle holders on the bottom measure 2" high. *Top candle holders courtesy of Walter Schirra Ceramics (calpottery@mindspring.com). Bottom candle holders courtesy of Naomi's of San Francisco.* Top: $90 pair; bottom: $165 pair

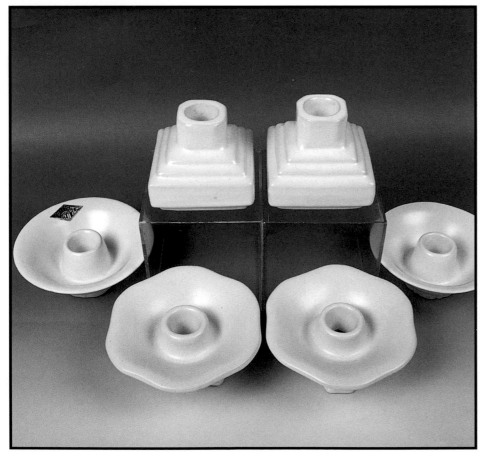

Six candle holders. The round candleholders measure 4.5" in diameter. *Courtesy of June Sakata Scoggins.* Top to bottom: $90 pair, $90 pair, $125 pair

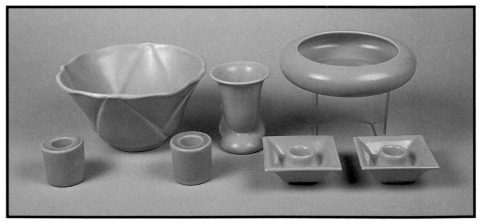

Artware bowls, vases, and candlesticks: bowls, 8" and 7.25" d.; vase, 4.25" h., round candlesticks (#855), 2" h.; square candlesticks. *Courtesy of June Sakata Scoggins.* Bowls and vases: $35-55; round candlesticks: $45 pair; square candlesticks: $20 each

Vase, 7.25" h.; candle holders (holding three candlesticks each), 7.5" l. *Courtesy of June Sakata Scoggins.* Vase: $55; candleholders: $75 pair

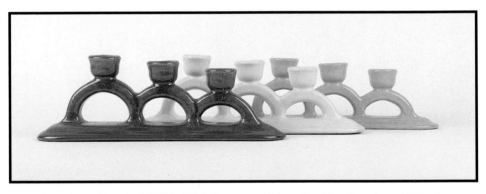

Console bowls (#4300) with a circular "Pacific Made In USA" mark, 12" d. x 3.5" h. *Courtesy of June Sakata Scoggins.* $65+

Blue vase, circular Pacific mark, 9.25" h.; two ballerina figurines (no numbers), circular stamped mark, 7" h.; and two candle holders (holding two candlesticks each), 6" w. *Courtesy of June Sakata Scoggins.* Vase: $65; ballerinas: $85 each; candle holders: $55 pair

Three branch candlesticks (#707), 10" l. *Courtesy of Naomi's of San Francisco.* $195 pair

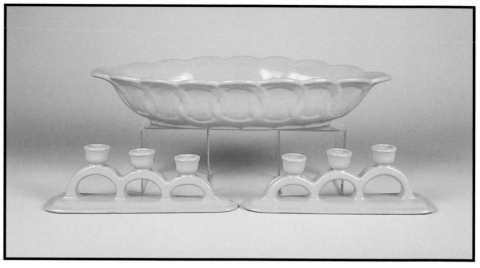

Console bowl and two candlesticks. Console bowl (#710), 16.75" l.; three branch candlesticks, 10" l. *Courtesy of Walter Schirra Ceramics (calpottery@mindspring.com)*. Console bowl: $125+; candlesticks: $195 pair

Yellow console bowl (#710) and two three branch candlesticks (#707). Console bowl, 16.75" l.; candlesticks, 10" l. *Courtesy of June Sakata Scoggins*. Bowl: $125+; candlesticks: $195 pair

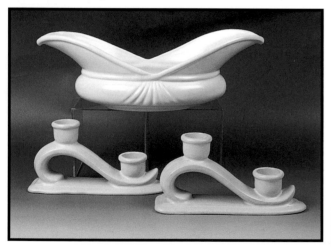

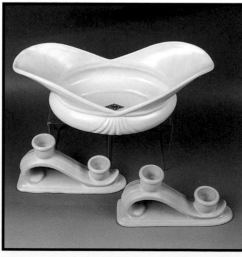

Bowl (#3609) and candle holders (with two holders each) (#711). Bowl: 11" l.; candle holders: 6.75" l. *Courtesy of June Sakata Scoggins*. Bowl: $95; candle holders: $65 pair

Low bowl (#3053) and leaf candlesticks. Bowl: 7" l.; candlesticks: 4.25" h. *Courtesy of June Sakata Scoggins*. Bowl: $75; candlesticks: $75 pair

Figurals and Floral Wares

Here are the figural pieces along with all of the artwares designed to contain and display flowers. Included are flower bowls, containers, frogs, pots, planters, and vases. Floor vases are not included here as they were designed to be displayed by themselves, rather than to display flowers!

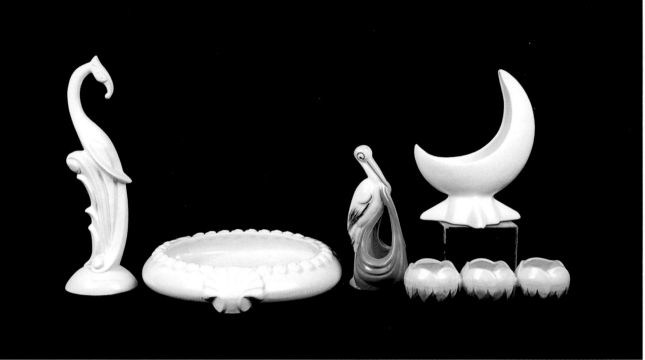

Figural planters/vases, 7.75" to 12.25" h.; three pot planter, 8" l. The tall stylized bird figural and the three pot planter were both identified with an ink stamped "Pacific Made In Calif. USA" manufacturer's mark. The rest of these pieces have molded "Pacific" circular manufacturer's marks. *Courtesy of June Sakata Scoggins.* Left to right: stylized bird: $95; low bowl: $65; stork flower bowl (#903): $125; half moon vase: $65; low triple planter: $35

Bird figural pieces: the white figures have three small tab feet while the more colorfully glazed example has no tab feet. All are marked with an ink stamp. 6.25" h. *Courtesy of June Sakata Scoggins.* $85 each

Parrot planters, indentified with molded circle mark, 14.5" l.; bird candle holders, 4.5" l. *Courtesy of June Sakata Scoggins.* Planters: $195+; candle holders: $95 set

Stork flower frog marked with a stamped circular "Pacific Made in Calif. USA" mark, 13.5" h. *Courtesy of Jerry Kunz.* $175

Swan planters in two sizes (#857 & #856) and candle holders (#859). 11" l., 6.5" l.; and 4" l. A circular "Pacific Made In USA" mark was used on the larger pieces and a simple linear "Pacific" mark on the candle holders. *Courtesy of Robert R. Perry.* #857: $70 each; #856: $55 each; #859: $30 each

Five bird vases, mold marked "Made in USA 3344," incised "R," and stamped with a circular "Pacific Made In Calif. USA" mark, 8" high each. *Courtesy of Jerry Kunz.* The cobalt glazed pair are valued $150+ for the pair. Single examples are valued $65+ each.

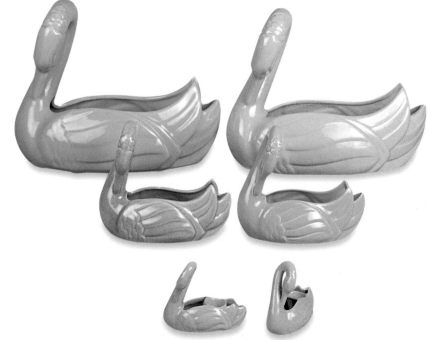

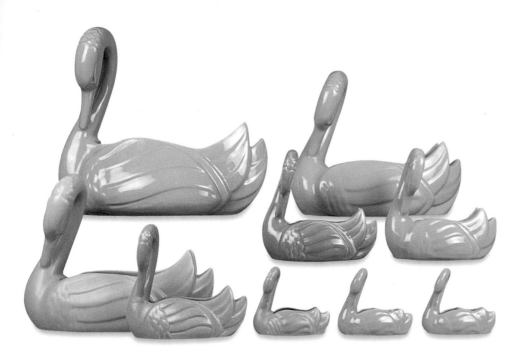

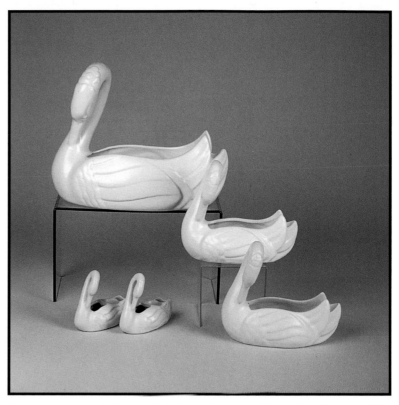

Swan planters and candle holders in four sizes, the bottom two on the right are the candle holders. Largest to smallest: #858, 12.5" l.; #857, #856, #883, and candle holders #639, 4" l. *Courtesy of June Sakata Scoggins.* $30 to $70+ each by size and type.

Swans in white, including candle holders. *Courtesy of June Sakata Scoggins.* $30 to $70+ each by size and type.

Additional swans. *Courtesy of June Sakata Scoggins.* $30 to $70+ each by size and type.

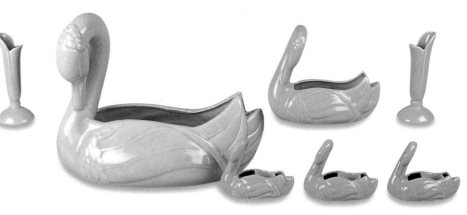

Swan planters, small swan flower and candle holders, and a pair of bud vases in leaf forms. Large swan (#858), unmarked, 12" l. x 10.5" h. Medium sized swan (#856) (also appears as a bank) is marked "856" with a circular "Pacific Made In USA" molded mark, 6.5" l. x 6" h. Small swans, marked with a "859 Pacific Made In USA" molded mark, 4.25" l. x 3.5" h. Bud vases, unmarked, 5.25" h. *Courtesy of Naomi's of San Francisco.* #858 swan: $75; #856 swan: $55; #859 swans: $30 each; bud vases: $65 pair

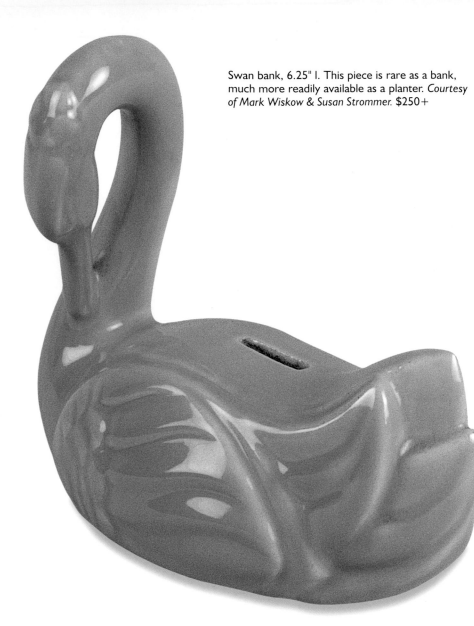

Swan bank, 6.25" l. This piece is rare as a bank, much more readily available as a planter. *Courtesy of Mark Wiskow & Susan Strommer.* $250+

Yes, deer! Tall and short deer figurals (no numbers), marked with a circular ink stamped "Pacific Made In Calif. USA" manufacturer's mark, 9" and 7" h. *Courtesy of June Sakata Scoggins.* 9"h.: $65; 7" h.: $45

Fish vases (#3338, #3110, and #3005), 7", 5.75", and 4.75" h. *Courtesy of June Sakata Scoggins.*
7" h.: $65; 5.75" h.: $55; 4.75" h.: $45

Bowl (#57) with fish flower frog and Madonna (#206) figural. Bowl: 15.5" l.; Madonna, 8" h. *Courtesy of June Sakata Scoggins.* Bowl: $85; flower frog: $95; Madonna: $125+

Madonna (#902), marked "902," 7.75" h.; small horse, unmarked, 4.5" l. *Courtesy of Jimm Edgar & Bettie Dakotah.* Madonna: $125; horse: $75+

White ballerina figurine, 7" h. *Courtesy of Walter Schirra Ceramics (calpottery@mindspring.com).* $95

157

Left: Jill (#906) and Jack (#907) flower bowls, marked with the circular Pacific mark in some cases, 5" h. *Courtesy of June Sakata Scoggins.* $65+ each

Right: Araminta plain and fancy skirt woman planters: plain (#900), fancy (#3201), all with either a circular "Pacific Made In USA" manufacturer's mark or nothing, all 7.5" h. *Courtesy of June Sakata Scoggins.* $65+ each

Left: George and Martha Washington planter and wall pockets. The wall pockets are rare and the dark green glazed wall pocket is very rare. Planter: 3060L and R; wall pockets: 3113 L and R, 6" l. each. *Courtesy of June Sakata Scoggins.* Matching sets: $65+; single pieces: $25+

Right: Figural salt and pepper shakers that straddle the line between artware and tableware. Farmer (#1066), 4.75" h.; farmer's wife (#1066), 4.25" h. These figures feature either R and L or S and P designations. Rooster and hen (#1073); lambs (#1071); elephants (#1070); pigs (#1074). *Courtesy of June Sakata Scoggins.* Sets: $75+ per set

Artware jardiniere, vase, and bowl, 9" h. x
10.5" d., 8" h. and 3" h. x 8" across. *Courtesy of
June Sakata Scoggins.* $55-75

Vase, bowl, and bud vase: vase (#1523), 8.5" h.; bowl
(#55), 8.5" d.; bud vase (#886), 7.25" h. All with circular
"Pacific Made In USA" marks. *Courtesy of June Sakata
Scoggins.* $45+ each

Flower and cactus pots ranging from 8.25" h. to 4" h. *Courtesy of June Sakata Scoggins.* Cactus: $225; flower pots: $45 to $85

Six sizes of flower pots, black stamp marked "Artware by Pacific Made in Calif. USA." These pots range in size from 8" to 3.5" h. *Courtesy of June Sakata Scoggins.* These pots range in value from $95 to $145.

Garden pots. Left pot is marked with molded "Pacific Made In USA 1564." Right pot is marked with a stamped "Art Ware Pacific Made in Calif. USA." 8.5" & 7.75" high respectively. *Courtesy of Jimm Edgar & Bettie Dakotah.* $75+ each

Light blue vase, 5.75" h.; small cobalt flower pot, 4.5" h. x 6" d. *Courtesy of Mark Wiskow & Susan Strommer.* Left to right: $45+, $75+

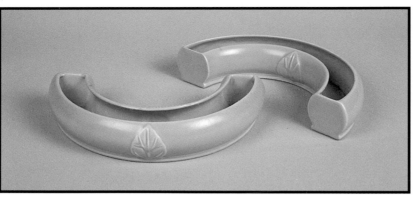

Half round planters (#719), 9" l. each, 9" d. when together. *Courtesy of Robert R. Perry.* $25+ each

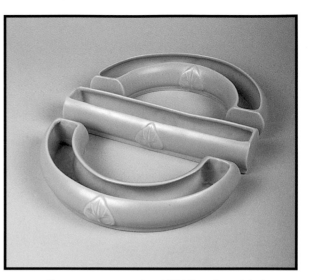

Planter set: center bar (#718) and semicircle (#719) planters. All are adorned with a single molded leaf decoration on either side. Molded "Pacific USA" and number marks. The center bar planter measures 8.5" in length. *Courtesy of June Sakata Scoggins.* $25 each

Planter (#1538), molded circular mark, 13" wide x 7.5" h. *Courtesy of June Sakata Scoggins.* $125

When Pacific jumped into the artware market in 1932, these Marigold vases were among their early offerings. Large Marigold vases (#808), 7" h.; small Marigold vase (#816), 5.25" h. *Courtesy of June Sakata Scoggins.* #808: $65 each; #816: $55

Opposite page
Top left: Marigold vases: flat Marigold vase (#808), unmarked, 8" h.; flat oblong Marigold vase (#816), 5" h. *Courtesy of Robert R. Perry.* #808: $65; #816: $55

Top right: Vase (#1504) and jardiniere (#1125), 12.5" h. and 9" h. *Courtesy of June Sakata Scoggins.* $145, $65

Bottom left: Two large vases. Left: vase (#1505) marked "1505 Pacific Made In USA," 15.5" h.; right: vase (#881) marked "881 Pacific Made In USA," 12.5" h. *Courtesy of Naomi's of San Francisco.* Left to right: $250+, $125

Bottom right: Two vases. Left: vase (#3603) marked "Pacific Made In USA 3603," 11.5" h.; right: vase (#833) marked "Pacific Made In USA 833," 8" h. *Courtesy of Naomi's of San Francisco.* $125 each

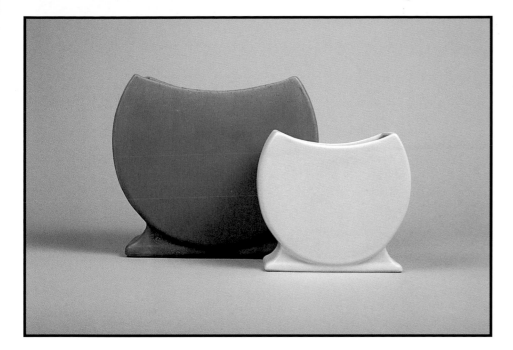

Prototype vase with experimental glaze, incised decoration, marked "T-736," 13" h. *Courtesy of Jimm Edgar & Bettie Dakotah.* $350+

Artware vases, 6.25" to 5.25" h. The top left example is earlier and is very heavy. *Courtesy of June Sakata Scoggins.* $65-95

A rare sample vase marked "Pacific Sample Sep 17 1941," 5.75" h. x 8" l. *Courtesy of Bill Stern (wbstern@aol.com).* $125+

Three handled vases (#800) with an impressed "800" only, 6" h. *Courtesy of June Sakata Scoggins.* $85 each

Vase (#64), marked with circular "Pacific Made In USA" mark, 15.5" h. *Courtesy of June Sakata Scoggins.* $350

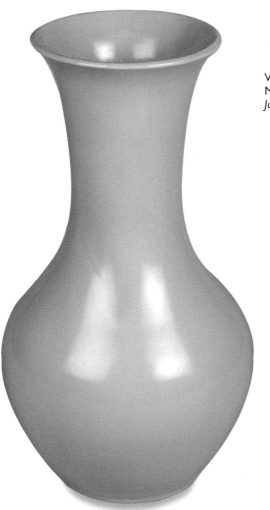

Left: ship's prow vase (#4000) with a circular "Pacific Made In USA" mark, 14" h. Right: white vase (#3807), with both circular molded and stamped manufacturer's marks, 11.5" h. The stamped mark reads "Pacific Made In Calif. USA." *Courtesy of June Sakata Scoggins.* Left to right: $150+, $95+

Large pastel green vase, 15.25" h. *Courtesy of Naomi's of San Francisco.* $400+

Three vases and two candle holders. The center shell vase (#3611) measures 8" h. x 10.5" w. The end vases (#3349) feature a molded manufacturer's mark reading "Made in USA" with the line number, and a stamped, circular ink mark "Pacific Made In Calif. USA," 7.5" h. The candleholders are marked with the ink stamped circle mark only, 4.25" h. *Courtesy of June Sakata Scoggins.* Shell vase: $150+; #3349 vases: $85+ each; candleholders: $85 pair

Artware: center shell base, marked with an odd "L" on the back, 13.5" l.; conch shell, 9" l.; and three additional vases. *Courtesy of June Sakata Scoggins.* $35-75 each

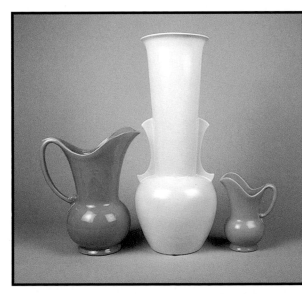

Three late vases: #3057 in white and two #3005s, one with a paper label. These vases feature late "Pacific USA" circular marks. *Courtesy of Robert R. Perry.* $45 each

Vase, 18" h., and two pitchers. *Courtesy of June Sakata Scoggins.* Vase: $150; pitchers: $45 and $35 respectively

Top left: A sampling of 1940s vases: the two on the left are #3348 and #3064 (the same style in 6.5" and 5" heights, both marked with "Made In USA" and the number only); top right red #3052 vase with a circular Pacific mark, 6.25" h.; lower right green #3006 vase marked "Pacific USA;" and bottom center loop handled #3015 vase, 3" h. *Courtesy of June Sakata Scoggins.* $35-55+ each

Top right: Two vases: the left vase is decorated with a molded floral motif and is identified with a "Pacific Pottery" paper label, marked "Pacific Made In USA 3052," 6.25" h.; the right vase is fish shaped, illegibly marked, 4.75" h. *Courtesy of Jerry Kunz.* $45+ each

168

Opposite page

Top left: Vases, 8.75" to 3.5" h.; and a three part planter, 8" l. *Courtesy of June Sakata Scoggins.* $25-55 each

Bottom left: Vases ranging from 10" to 6" h. and a planter, 9.25" l. *Courtesy of June Sakata Scoggins.* $35-55 each

Top right: Vases in order: #3101, 7" h.; #3009, 5" h.; #3106, 7" h. *Courtesy of June Sakata Scoggins.* Left to right: $95, $45, $85

Bottom right: Artware vases and candle holder, 12.75" to 3.75" h. *Courtesy of June Sakata Scoggins.* These pieces range in value from $35 to $85.

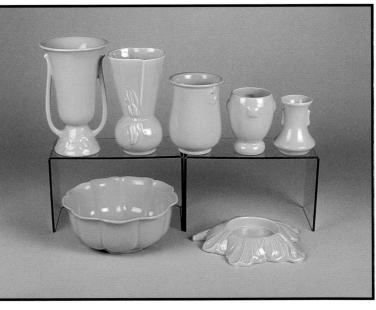

Top left: Artware vases, ranging from 10.5" to 2.5" h. *Courtesy of June Sakata Scoggins.* These vases range in value from $35 to $95.

Top right: Vases and bowl: vases, 8.5" to 4" h.; bowl, 10.75" l. *Courtesy of June Sakata Scoggins.* These items range in value from $25 to $125.

Bottom left: Vases and bowl: vases: 7.75" to 4" h.; bowl: 8" l. *Courtesy of June Sakata Scoggins.* These items range in value from $15 to $75.

Botom right: Vases, bowl, and stand: vases, 8.25" h. to 4" h.; bowl (#55), circular Pacific mark, 8.5" d.; stand, ink stamped mark "Pacific Made In Calif. USA," 8.5" l. *Courtesy of June Sakata Scoggins.* These items range in value from $25 to $85.

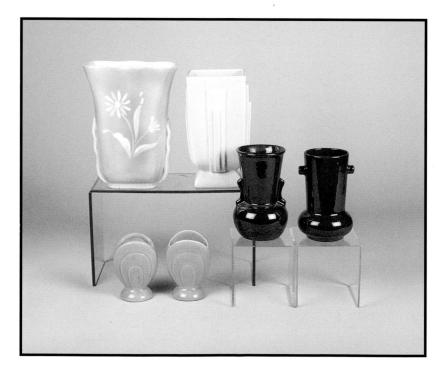

Top left: Vases and a shell bowl: vases: 9.5" to 4.5" h.; shell bowl, 7" l. *Courtesy of June Sakata Scoggins.* These items range in value from $15 to $85.

Bottom left: Vases: top: #3341, #3107; center: two red unmarked vases; bottom: two #3012. These vases range in height from 7.25 to 3.75" h. *Courtesy of June Sakata Scoggins.* These items range in value from $45 to $65.

Top right: Vases, 10.25" to 4" h. and a console bowl, 10.25" d. The red vases are #3003 and #3002. *Courtesy of June Sakata Scoggins.* These pieces range in value from $25 to $125.

Bottom right: Artware vases ranging from 10.5" h. to 4" h. in air brushed multiple glaze colors. *Courtesy of June Sakata Scoggins.* These items range in value from $35 to $65.

Sand Jars / Umbrella Stands

These pieces were best suited for public spaces. Sand jars were convenient places to stub out and deposit cigarette butts.

Two green sand jars, 20.5" h. Rare. *Courtesy of Mark Wiskow & Susan Strommer.* $600+ each

Red or burgundy sand jar. 20.5" h. Rare. *Courtesy of Mark Wiskow & Susan Strommer.* $750+

Two cobalt sand jars (#1106) in the "Deco Skyscraper" motif, 20.5" h. Rare. *Courtesy of Mark Wiskow & Susan Strommer.* $600+ each

Orange and yellow sand jars. *Courtesy of Mark Wiskow & Susan Strommer.* $600+ each

Two green sand jars comparing the "Deco Skyscraper" and banded (#1131) motifs. Rare. *Courtesy of Mark Wiskow & Susan Strommer.* $600+ each

Cobalt ribbed corset shape sand jar (#1117) with three sets of 1/2 round rings, 26" h. *Courtesy of Mark Wiskow & Susan Strommer.* $1200+

White umbrella stand, 14.5" h. *Courtesy of Walter Schirra Ceramics (calpottery@mindspring.com).* $1050+

Vases

Presented here is an impressive array of large floor vases.

Large cobalt floor vases (#1112), 32 & 34" h. *Courtesy of Jerry Kunz.* $1850+ each

Large floor vase (#1112), 32" h. *Courtesy of June Sakata Scoggins.* $1850+

Large floor vases (#1100A), marked with circular "Pacific Made In USA" mark, 24" h. *Courtesy of June Sakata Scoggins.* $1200+ each

173

Two floor vases, 21" h. *Left: courtesy of Jerry Kunz. Right: courtesy of Walter Schirra Ceramics (calpottery@mindspring.com)*. $850+ each

Floor vases, orange, 24" h. *Courtesy of Jimm Edgar & Bettie Dakotah*. $1800+ pair; $850+ each

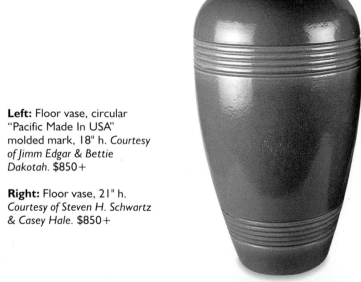

Left: Floor vase, circular "Pacific Made In USA" molded mark, 18" h. *Courtesy of Jimm Edgar & Bettie Dakotah.* $850+

Right: Floor vase, 21" h. *Courtesy of Steven H. Schwartz & Casey Hale.* $850+

BIBLIOGRAPHY

"Big Gain Reported in N.Y. Pottery and Glass Sales." *Ceramic Industry,* January 1935.

"Buying Continues Active at Los Angeles, Chicago." *Ceramic Industry,* March 1942, pp. 46-48, 53.

"California Sun-Kissed Pottery Made in Modern Plant. Pacific Clay Products, Inc., Producer of Structural Clay Products, Has Entered the Pottery Field with a Line of Distinctive Ware." *Ceramic Industry,* September 1935, pp. 131-132.

Chipman, Jack. *Collector's Encyclopedia of California Pottery.* Second Edition. Paducah, Kentucky: Collector Books, 1999.

"Colored Pottery. California Manufacturers Lead the World in Beauty of Design and Coloring." *California—Magazine of Pacific Business,* September 1937, pp. 16-19, 39-42.

Cox, Lucille T. "A Little Glimpse Here and There in the E. Liverpool Potteries." *Ceramic Industry,* June 1942, p. 38.

Gibney, Raymond G. "Best Business in Year '42 Pittsburgh Show." *Ceramic Industry,* February 1942, pp. 34-35.

Kaeppel, H.V. "The Roving Reporter on the West Coast," *Ceramic Industry,* November 1937, p. 358-359.

_____. "The Roving Reporter on the West Coast," *Ceramic Industry,* February 1938, pp. 62-63.

"Making the Rounds of the Markets. Los Angeles. Reports from the Summer Gift and Art Shows." *Ceramic Industry,* September 1940, p. 46.

"Pacific." *New West,* August 14, 1978, p. 71.

"Pacific Clay Busy On Insulating Pieces." *Ceramic Industry,* October 1942.

"Pacific Clay Continues 7 Dinnerware Patterns." *Ceramic Industry,* August 1942.

"Pacific Clay Shows Higher Earnings." *Ceramic Industry,* April 1929.

"Pacific Clay Products Builds New Shop." *Ceramic Industry,* September 1942.

"Pacific Clay Products Streamlines Office." *Ceramic Industry,* July 1942, p. 40.

"Pacific Distributes Art Ware Through Jobber." *Ceramic Industry,* June 1942.

"Pacific Introduces Bright New Accents in Pottery . . ." *American Home,* October 1937.

"Pacific Prepares Its 1942 Lines." *Ceramic Industry,* October 1941, p. 25.

"Pacific Southwest Exposition, Long Beach, Cal., July 27 to September 3: Pacific Clay Products Company's booth." *Ceramic Industry,* September 1928.

"Pastels and Ivory in New Decorative Pieces." *Arts & Decorations,* April 1935.

Snyder, Jeffrey B. *Beautiful Bauer: A Pictorial Study with Prices.* Atglen, Pennsylvania: Schiffer Publishing, 2001.

_____. *Depression Pottery.* Atglen, Pennsylvania: Schiffer Publishing, 1999.

_____. *Fiesta. Homer Laughlin China Company's Colorful Dinnerware.* Atglen, Pennsylvania: Schiffer Publishing, 2000 (3rd Edition).

_____. *Franciscan Dining Services.* Atglen, Pennsylvania: Schiffer Publishing, 1996.

_____. *McCoy Pottery.* Atglen, Pennsylvania: Schiffer Publishing, 1999.

"Two Structural Clay Products Firms Make Success at Pottery." *Ceramic Industry,* May 1935, p. 71.

Wiskow, Mark. Personal Notes. 1999.

INDEX